Soviet Style *in* Management

Soviet Style *in* Management

Nathan Leites

Foreword by Andrew Marshall

Crane Russak · *New York*

Soviet Style in Management

Published in the United States by
Crane, Russak & Company, Inc.
3 East 44th Street
New York, NY 10017

ISBN 0-8448-1490-3

Library of Congress Cataloging in Publication Data

Leites, Nathan Constantin, 1912–
Soviet style in management.

Bibliography: p.
Includes index.
1. Management—Soviet Union. 2. Industrial management —Soviet Union. 3. Kommunisticheskaia partiia Sovetskogo Soviuza. 4. Work ethic—Soviet Union. I. Title.
HD70.S63L44 1985 658.'00947 85-4686
ISBN 0-8448-1490-3 (pbk.)

Printed in the United States of America

CONTENTS

FOREWORD vii
Andrew Marshall

PREFACE ix

SUMMARY xiii

Chapter

I. INACTION (*BEZDEISTVIE*) 1
The Party's Leading Role 1
Activeness (*Aktivnost'*) 4
Surge (*Pod'em*) 18
Duty (*Dolg*) 30
Material Stimulation 40
Kontrol' 51

II. NOT GOING TO THE END (*BROSIT' NA POLPUTI*) 58

III. SCATTERING (*RASPYLENIE*) 77

IV. INTERMITTENCE (*PRERYVISTOST'*) 80

V. WASTING TIME 83

VI. FAILURE TO CALCULATE (*NEPRODUMANNOST'*) 89

VII. UNEVENNESS (*NEROVNOST'*) 97

VIII. LACK OF COHESION (*RAZOBSHCHENNOST'*) 101

IX. SUPERIORS' RAGE AND REMOTENESS (*GRUBOST', BEZUCHAST'NOST'*) 107

X. FEAR AND FEAR OF FEAR (*STRAKH*) 109

REFERENCES 111

INDEX 113

SELECTED LIST OF RAND BOOKS 117

FOREWORD

Nathan Leites has produced another in what is now a long line of distinguished analyses of Soviet modes of thinking, patterns of behavior, and casts of mind. As always in his work, it is based on the analysis of a great deal of material but is very economical in its presentation of findings. Inferred conclusions are largely left to the reader, but meticulous care has been taken to suggest the special way in which words have been used by the Soviets and hence reflect distinctive concerns, fears, or ways of looking at the world. Reading Leites requires special efforts on the part of the reader. However, because of the care with which the quotations have been selected, and the special features of what the Soviets are saying about various aspects of managing the Soviet society and economy, close reading is well rewarded.

As mentioned in the Preface, this analysis is a companion, or civilian counterpart, to Leites' previous analysis of *Soviet Style in War.* What is striking when the two analyses are compared is the prominence of some of the same themes. In Chapter 1 of *Soviet Style in War*—"Warding Off Inaction"—the themes of inaction, "not going to the end" and "scattering," are very prominent. In the military analysis, the theme is "warding off slowness"; in the present (civilian) analysis, the focus is on "pausing" and "wasting time" as discrete themes. Similar parallels occur with the other major military themes of "lack of cohesion" and "failure to calculate." Where distinctive differences appear between the two analyses, they arise because war is a competitive, two-sided activity in which one has to be concerned not only with the actions of one's own forces, but also with those of the opponent. The themes that arise in *Soviet Style in War* are, therefore, focused in some cases on injunctions to enhance one's own cohesion and reduce that of the enemy, or on improving one's capacity to calculate while degrading that of the enemy. Also, certain concerns arise with respect to "slowness" and "pausing" because of the fear that the enemy may be quicker or less inclined to pause and do nothing.

Nonetheless, in both cases—in managing forces in combat and in managing the society and economy—there is a pervasive distrust of ordinary human beings, of human nature, and perhaps of what seem to the Soviet leadership to be distinctive attributes of the human material that makes up the mass of Soviet society. Many of these concerns and fears are not special to the Soviet Union or to the Soviet leaders, of course. Heads of large organizations everywhere doubtless share many of these concerns about the people under them. What Leites is pointing out is the degree to which these concerns are heightened and salient in the thinking, and reflected in the practices, of the Soviet leadership. Moreover, even if some of the concerns are shared by leaders in other countries, it is unlikely that those leaders would voice them so baldly and so repetitively in print, especially in widely circulated newspapers and journals.

The Party's anxiety about the natural inclination of the masses and of the lower levels of management, as well as its inclinations toward an active role for itself and the kinds of measures it deems necessary for the economy to operate effectively, raises questions about its willingness to accept, or to trust, the economic reforms favored by economists. Decentralization, trust in the spontaneous activity of workers and lower and middle management, does not fit well with these concerns and inclinations. Leites' works suggest to me the acute difficulties that lie in the way of efforts at reform of the Communist system through the use of the marketplace.

Andrew Marshall
Washington, D.C.
February 1985

PREFACE

This is the final report of a project sponsored by the Director of Net Assessment, Office of the Secretary of Defense. It furnishes a civilian counterpart to a previous project whose ultimate form was a book, *Soviet Style in War*, Crane, Russak & Company, Inc., 1982. The themes developed here should be of interest to analysts of the dispositions of the Soviet leadership.

The points made in this volume are drawn from the words of Soviet leaders and from three publications close to the Kremlin: *Pravda* (daily), 1980 to date; *Kommunist* (fortnightly), 1970 to date; and *Partiinaya Zhizn'* (*Party Life*) (fortnightly), 1970 to date. The publications are cited by the short forms *P*, *K*, and *PZh*, respectively.

None of the quoted statements about Soviet life made here is to be attributed to the present author. It is always the Kremlin that is speaking, often alleging what it hardly believes or betraying what it did not intend to disclose.

Of course, the present author does not affirm that, in reality or according to the leadership, the dispositions alluded to in the chapter headings are present only in the Soviet Union. A guess is merely this: the Soviet leadership attributes a higher rate of occurrence and a more negative impact to these dispositions than do many Western leaderships to the same dispositions in *their* societies.

Even when the author of a statement quoted has a position far below the Soviet top, his being printed in the publications named makes it probable that what he is saying is desired to be stated at a high level.

Does the Kremlin believe what it declares? Surely much less than fully, and probably much more than not at all. The ambiguity as well as the self-serving nature of many of the points to be discussed facilitate a measure of belief. In any case, the Kremlin's choice of pretense may permit a guess of what is really on its mind.

During the Brezhnev era and the first half-year of Andropov's regime, the Kremlin varied little in its expressions on the matters discussed below. This fact usually goes unacknowledged; one will often advance a hoary point as if it had never been made before.

The vanity of repetition may in a rare instance be admitted when one deals with a small affair well below the top:

> The primary Party organization issued a strong blame for K. Sisov. But the lesson, as one says, did not profit him. Sisov continued. . . . There were conversations with him "off the record" and at the session of the Party Bureau; attention was directed to his unworthy conduct. However, he disregarded that. . . . But even that punishment did not change his conduct.[1]

But it is very rare to see it observed that "for many years we have been talking about the same defects, and there is no change."[2] Unless there is change—Brezhnev once threatened, when urging that certain decisions be implemented—"we shall be forced to return every year to the same questions."[3] Yet it is unusual for a protest against this actually happening decade after decade to become public.

> Some regular (*shtatnyi'*) speakers . . . keep old texts. They enter the new names of advanced workers, and the speech is ready. You sit there, you listen to the speakers reading similar speeches, real twins.[4]

> I had to attend various conferences and meetings. You sit sometimes in the hall, you listen to the speaker and . . . think: yesterday, the day before yesterday, even earlier, the same words resounded here. . . . Sometimes one senses the urge to get up and say, "Stop, comrades! We have already talked and overtalked of this. Let us leave and simply do what we have decided!" To be sure, I did not get up; I did not say this.[5]

It is even rare to note calmly that "the agenda of plenums, sessions of the Party bureau and meetings often repeat themselves from year to year,"[6] as it is unusual to argue that "there is no ground for concern about our repeating ourselves with regard to the same questions."[7] Goodness of content, it may be argued, justifies, even requires, repetition. "This truth is not new, but there is no harm in repeating it."[8] "One may say that these are well-known truths. Nevertheless, it is useful to recall them."[9] "This theme is far from being exhausted, and it becomes necessary to write about it almost in the same tone as before,

---

[1]N. Minaev, *PZh,* 1980, No. 5, p. 69.

[2]A Party member, quoted in Yu. Zhigailov, *P,* October 10, 1980.

[3]At the Central Committee Plenum, November 1979, quoted by N. Shvats, *PZh,* 1980, No. 9, p. 37.

[4]V. Krushevskii, *P,* July 14, 1982.

[5]V. Lebedeva, *P,* January 14, 1982.

[6]Editorial, *P,* February 11, 1982.

[7]A. Pelshe 1978, p. 405.

[8]V. Ivanov, *P,* February 25, 1981.

[9]L. Kravchuk, *P,* February 10, 1982.

to bring forward similar proofs."[10] "Must one speak of these principles in detail? Would this not be an unnecessary repetition of known truths? No, to repeat that which is known and important . . . is necessary . . . for action."[11]

It needed no less a spokesman than Andropov to declare his refusal to repeat the obvious: "I shall not dwell at length on the need to complete the agricultural year successfully, to preserve the gathered harvest, to do the groundwork for next year's harvest, and to ensure successful livestock wintering. All this goes without saying."[12]

As a result of repetition, there is for many themes an abundance of specimens, often identical even in wording—a fact that made it possible for the present choice of illustrations often to be arbitrary. Sometimes an obscure name appears in a credit line where a famous one might have been presented.

On some prominent subjects the present author found nothing worth advancing (or repeating). Thus he does not deal with "moral stimulation" or "socialist competition" in Chap. I.

To present a fuller portrait of Soviet style in management, many other kinds of data besides those inspected below would have to be considered; and other researchers may perceive what escaped the author in the data with which he deals.

Whenever—as is mostly the case—themes opposing those presented below are left unmentioned, they have seemed of low weight. (They might turn out to be significant in non-Party publications.)

The author benefited from comments by Charles Wolf, Jr., and the assistance of Lubov Fajfer Wong. Unless otherwise noted, emphases in the text are the author's.

The author is a consultant to The Rand Corporation.

---

[10] I. Sharov, *P*, July 3, 1981.

[11] A. Pelshe, *K*, 1981, No. 11, p. 12.

[12] Central Committee Plenum, November 22, 1982, FBIS, November 23, p. R-5.

SUMMARY

In the Kremlin's public view, one of the main activities of the Party is its leadership of the economy. The Party not only determines rules and plans for production but also continuously influences daily economic activities down to the smallest economic units. The Party's all-encompassing participation in economic activities is, of course, alleged by the Kremlin to be a necessary or even a sufficient condition of economic success. Economic success or failure at various levels is said to be directly related to the participation of Party organizations in educational, ideological, and organizational activities. By discovering "reserves" and using them, Party organizations, supported by economic, technical, and engineering services, ensure the fulfillment of plans.

A major objective of the Party is maintaining and enhancing the population's "activeness" at all levels. The leading role in maintaining and enhancing activeness is delegated to Party cadres, in the face of a tendency to slide toward inaction. The tendency toward reduced activeness is a problem among the cadres themselves. Many of their activities, on the managerial or even the ministry level, are for appearance only and hide inaction. It is, therefore, an objective of the Party to increase activeness among its cadres, for it is believed that the performance of the masses is directly related to that of the cadres. One often talks about the "inexhaustible energy of the masses"; but it is the Party's private belief that the process to increase activeness begins at the top and spreads downward, channeling the "energy of the masses."

Higher activeness, it is believed, may be the result of a heightened mood at work which then leads to increased productivity. High efficiency of work can be achieved by "inspiring" the working masses. By improving conditions of life and work, the Party strives to influence the mood of the workers in the hope of more efficient performance. Party cadres are charged with being aware of the mood of "work collectives." The aim is to create a mood of "being carried away" (*pod'em*), where all energy is directed toward the fulfillment of tasks. The Party cadres seem to be aware of and dismayed by widespread aversion toward work. In creating the mood of *pod'em*, the Party strives to change the natural inclination of an ordinary person to lead an "easy" life and to produce in that person a need for challenge, where he not only does not avoid strenuous and painstaking work, but in fact cannot live without it.

To quote Chernenko: "In socialist society an attitude of initiative toward work becomes the first existential need of man, a moral norm."

Before work can become a need, it is said, it must become a habit. To achieve this goal the Party declares work to be one's obligation (*dolg*) toward society, hoping that combining the feelings of *dolg* and *pod'em* will have the desired result. In the meantime, the leadership is faced with the fact that personnel on all levels have few compunctions about disregarding the requirements of their jobs or the orders of their superiors. The treatment of this topic suggests the prevalence of such violations, and almost their moral acceptability. Under these conditions, elementary obligations of workers are raised to the level of being meritorious or innovative. Thus the Party, in spite of its professed hope, cannot rely on *dolg* as a major motive for work by the "masses."

The Kremlin acknowledges that "to build communism only on the enthusiasm of toilers is a utopia" and reluctantly demands that income should depend on performance, that "every worker should see and feel the connection between what he has done and what he has earned" (Brezhnev). But the use of economic incentives is counteracted by reliance on the previously discussed motivations more congenial to the Kremlin. The Kremlin's support of economic incentives is limited by its belief that such a reliance might lead to losing, or at least might make hard to justify, the Party's "leading role" in the economy.

Recognizing the limits of *pod'em* and "material stimulation," the Party affirms relying on *kontrol'*—surveillance and correction of one's performance by others—to achieve high performance. It is not excluded that high performance may exist under conditions of low *kontrol'*, but such situations will not be permanent. Low performance is usually attributed to low level of *kontrol'*, and the degree of fulfillment of designated tasks is directly related to the degree of *kontrol'* exercised. The aim of the Party is said to be to "create a system of control in which the very concept of 'nonexecution of adopted decisions' would become impossible"; that is, the Party suggests that *kontrol'* is also a means to strengthen the sense of *dolg*. It would seem to follow that the need for *kontrol'* should decline, the longer it has been exercised in a given situation. This implication, however, is never drawn. *Kontrol'* is in fact designed to cover a persisting defect—to achieve by fear what conscience should, but will not, accomplish. The cadres entrusted with implementing *kontrol'* are often charged with using it insufficiently, formally, and merely for show, which in turn results in unfulfilled goals (Chap. I).

The Party is aware that often collectives do not complete an operation, but stop somewhere along the line. This seems to occur frequently enough to induce the wishful comment that the "activeness of most Party committees is characterized by the aspiration to complete projects." And "the ability to bring what has been started to a conclusion," becomes "the main quality of the Party leader." The Party insists on "Bolshevik stubbornness" in attaining objectives, emphasizing that attaining any important objective is likely to take a long time and require much work. One should complete tasks already started before proceeding to new ones. Some operations, it is regularly said, go no further than the discussion stage. At times, Party organizations consider meetings "as the chief criterion of productive work." It seems appropriate to insist that "the most passionate discourses on exactingness and personal responsibility cannot replace real exactingness and effective demandingness" (Chap. II).

There is an inclination, the Party leadership discerns, toward scattering resources over multiple objectives, thus reducing productivity—that is, an inability to concentrate efforts on the most important task. To counteract the inclination to scatter, the Party urges concentration—that is, applying large amounts of resources of all kinds to a given issue, in every domain. A crucial task is to discover in any situation the "main link," concentration on which will produce a much higher yield than any alternative choice. The capacity to concentrate, like activeness, flows downward from the Central Committee through the several levels of the Party to the masses (Chap. III).

There is a disposition among ordinary human beings to act intermittently and thus to degrade productivity, the maximum of which requires "uninterruptedness" of operation. The Party, therefore, stresses the requirement that every task be given an uninterrupted effort; work on any task should be conducted systematically and continuously rather than sporadically. "Uninterruptedness" becomes a modifier of any good development, as, for example, with regard to Marxism-Leninism as an "uninterruptedly developing doctrine" (Chap. IV).

There is a penchant to delay acting and, once one has begun, to act slowly, both of which make for low productivity. Instead of being late to begin, then working at a low level until rising to a crash effort when a deadline is near, there should (the Party leadership demands) be steadiness in operations, begun early and completed in good time. The Party stresses punctuality in fulfilling any goal, making decisions without wasting time, at times even trading the completeness of information for the sake of making a decision "in good time." Being on time is considered a point of excellence. Being ahead of time is even more desirable, for it carries an assurance that one is not losing speed, not coming to a standstill (Chap. V).

There is an inclination to engage in actions without an internally coherent, "concrete," and complete calculation. To this the Party leadership opposes the requirement of orienting every detail of an operation toward the final result sought. There is also a penchant for setting objectives that are unattainable with the resources at hand, for establishing plans without an analysis of real possibilities; the leadership explains that acting within one's means is preferable. To the disposition to improvise, the Party top opposes the requirement to prepare (Chap. VI).

To reduce the shifting of cadres to a minimum is a major objective, for such actions have a disruptive effect on performance. Personnel are likely to go from one extreme to the other in the course of an operation whose optimal conduct requires "evenness" in a "calm spirit" (Chap. VII).

The members of a work collective tend to be indifferent and even hostile to each other; obtaining a high yield from common work, however, requires feeling and acting as one. It is up to the Party to prevent the disastrous outcome of "things being left to themselves" by creating a collective that is highly productive because of the good feelings that prevail within it. To counteract the tendency for a collective to disintegrate, the Party promotes norms favoring cohesion. The "brigade" system, operating on the principle of collective responsibility for defective performance, is one example. Mutual responsibility is to be combined with mutual help, which contributes to good feelings within the collective (Chap. VIII).

Superiors, although apt to be remote from their subordinates and to rage against them if they are deemed defenseless, are inclined to sacrifice the interests of the cause to the risk of displeasing those who might retaliate (Chap. IX). Possessed by many fears, converging on the one of being annihilated, the Kremlin fears fear and inhibits its expression (Chap. X).

Chapter I

INACTION (*BEZDEISTVIE*)

THE PARTY'S LEADING ROLE

"When our Party came to rule," one may observe in an unusual feat of recall, "the leadership of the economy became its main activity." And today the Party still "requires of itself to lead the economy."[1] (What "the Party" and "to lead the economy" mean in this formulation may become clearer in the pages below.)

To lose this particular application of the Party's "leading role" is to lose that role itself. The "enemies of communism" know this and hence "strive to demonstrate the necessity to separate the Communist Parties of the socialist countries . . . from the leadership of the economy. . . . "[2]

But "unswervingly . . . the Communist Party considers the economy as the most important sphere of its . . . activity";[3] "leading the economy is the core of the Party's entire activity."[4]

Not only does the Party determine the *rules* and *plans* that are to govern economic personnel from unskilled worker to director of an association—although that function is necessary, it would not be sufficient—but the Party also, in aspiration and in allegation, massively "interferes" in the economy by a host of *particular* actions.

The Party should and does "*penetrate deeply* into the economy."[5] "To search for new reserves of economic growth"—which are apt to be located "in the depths"—"and to bring them into action is today the basis of bases in the activity of all Party organizations. . . . "[6]

Nothing, it is insisted, should be viewed as outside the scope of Party action. "There is no matter which communists have a right to brush aside: 'This does not concern us.' Everything concerns us!"[7]

---

[1]N. Konevalov, *K*, 1970, No. 12, p. 35.

[2]I. Kapitonov, *K*, 1972, No. 3, p. 30.

[3]P. Shelest, *K*, 1971, No. 12, p. 17.

[4]L. Brezhnev, speech at the 26th Party Congress, February 23, 1981, Brezhnev 1981a, p. 668.

[5]S. Medunov, *PZh*, 1979, No. 12, p. 18. Emphasis added.

[6]L. Brezhnev, at the Central Committee plenum of November 1978, quoted by A. Murashov, *PZh*, 1979, No. 4, p. 59.

[7]Editorial, *P*, October 15, 1982.

The Party's interventions should be, and are, not only *numerous* but also *continuous*. (See below, Chap. IV.) "The Party organization . . . influences the work collectives' activity daily."[8] "Party control over the economy consists precisely in the daily exercise of influence . . . on the life of production."[9]

The Party's role in the economy is not only "leading" but still rising as the economy's scale and complexity increase. "The center of Party work . . . shifts ever more to production."[10] It is only "during the last years that the system of means of struggle adopted by the Government against manifestations of *vedomstvennost'* [bureaucratism] began to need the daily support of the Party. . . . "[11] So far from the passage of time under "real socialism" reducing the need for such daily support, that need is rising (a highly convenient and hence probably not wholly insincere contention).

It is all-encompassing and minute intervention by the Party which is presented as surely a necessary and perhaps a sufficient condition of economic success. It is "thanks to the work of Party organizations" that the agricultural enterprises in a province "obtained positive results."[12] If the Moscow Association *Krasnyi Bogatyr* "has worked well during the period of the last Five-Year Plan . . . one of the most important causes of its success . . . was that all essential questions concerning it were constantly at the center of attention of the Party organizations."[13] It is indeed "the primary Party organizations . . . which secure the fulfillment and overfulfillment of production plans"; they "discover and utilize new reserve [means for enhancing production—NL], obtain a wide adoption of attainments of science and technology . . ., enhance the productivity of labor, [and] improve the quality of products."[14] Thus "the secret of the success of advanced [work] collectives is that *Party* organizations . . . organize . . . the work . . . supported by the economic, engineering, and technical services."[15] "The realization of the economic policy of the Party—the most important task of Party organizations": so runs the title of an editorial.[16]

The degree of that realization varies with Party performance. When an economic outcome is unfavorable, look for a deficiency in the

---

[8]G. Smaglienko, *PZh,* 1979, No. 5, p. 40.

[9]G. Pavlov, *K,* 1972, No. 4, p. 20.

[10]Editorial, *PZh,* 1980, No. 16, p. 20.

[11]M. Mikhailov, *K,* 1981, No. 8, p. 104.

[12]A. Titov and V. Kozyrenko, *PZh,* 1978, No. 15, p. 14.

[13]V. Grishin, *K,* 1981, No. 8, p. 11.

[14]G. Krivoshein, *PZh,* 1979, No. 16, p. 38.

[15]Editorial, *K,* 1981, No. 1, p. 7. Emphasis added.

[16]*PZh,* 1981, No. 4, p. 3.

Party's contribution: "And 'The causes of this? Which are they?' asked the communists. They arrived at the same conclusion: the influence of the Party on many sides of the life of the collective had weakened."[17] "Still recently the Lenin District [in the city] occupied one of the last places in the Province with regard to the majority of [production] indicators. . . . The cause of its lagging behind was that the District Committee of the Party . . . its bureau, the secretaries . . . did not show the appropriate initiative, stubbornness and exactingness. It became necessary to remove the first secretary of the District Committee and some other workers. Now the situation in the District has gradually improved."[18]

Intervening in the economy, Party cadres supposedly do not do the kind of work that economic managers are performing (there should be no "substitution" of Party for economic officials) but rather a different thing of which only Party cadres are capable. What it is often remains obscure under the guise of familiar objectives. "Economic problems are solved by the Party above all," one may indicate with a deceptive appearance of clarity due to the power of a word, "through *organizational* activities."[19] "Almost a year has passed since the resolution by the Central Committee of the Communist Party of the Soviet Union (CPSU) . . . on the perfecting of the economic mechanism; a certain amount of work in the direction indicated has been conducted [by economic officials and managers]. But all this activity lacks aim-directedness [see Chap. VI], energy [see next section]. For this work is . . . not reinforced by . . . *organizational* and *ideological* work [by the Party]. . . . Therefore, the results are not always satisfying."[20] "While we recognize the positive changes that have occurred in construction, we hold that our builders still do not work to the full measure of their possibilities"—because they lack the distinctive contribution of the Party. "Practice shows: where the primary Party organizations . . . occupy themselves with questions of production activity and conduct . . . *ideological-educational* work, there things go well."[21]

Such work, we are not surprised to hear, is not only of *decisive* importance, it is of *increasingly* decisive importance: "Building the economy depends ever more . . . on political-educational work"[22]—by the Party, to be sure.

---

[17]A. Zolin, *P*, November 28, 1981.

[18]V. Makarenko, *PZh*, 1979, No. 23, p. 47.

[19]Unsigned article, *PZh*, 1979, No. 14, pp. 21–22. Emphasis added.

[20]Editorial, *K*, 1980, No. 9, p. 5. Emphasis added.

[21]S. Medunov, *PZh*, 1979, No. 12, p. 15. Emphasis added.

[22]Editorial, *K*, 1980, No. 9, p. 6.

It is rare for the Party's contribution to an economic result to be publicly separated from the effects of other factors and then assessed modestly, as in one case of sharply increased production: "Naturally, much has been attained because of reconstruction and the introduction of advanced technology. But there was also something else: there operated that 'moral supplement' which was introduced into the collective by the efforts of the communities."[23] Usually, of course, the impression conveyed or allowed is that without such efforts there would not be much of a chance.

The more the Party top level and the Party cadres perceive doubts about the Party's economic role around them, and perhaps even among them, the more apt they are to insist on that role—as an antidote not only to losing some of their power and privilege, but perhaps to losing all.

But if the Party is interested in appearing to rescue the economy, it is equally interested in the economy seeming unable to run by itself; it is thus dependent to a degree on the arrangements making for such an incapacity *not* being "reformed."

ACTIVENESS (*AKTIVNOST'*)

The Party aims at maintaining/enhancing activeness (*aktivnost'*); it is at all times "struggling to raise everybody's activeness in work and in society."[24] "An active position in life (*aktivnaya zhiznenaya pozitsia*)" is the Kremlin's only formula for virtue at large.

Any presentation of a state of affairs as favorable is likely to show a rising activeness. "In our factory the activeness of the communists rises unswervingly."[25] "The activeness of the staffs of the Province Committee, the City Committees, and the District Committees has risen."[26] "The activeness of the [Soviet] people . . . is rising from year to year."[27]

Activeness, it may be taken for granted, is the principal aspect of a good event. "The meeting proceeded with unusual activeness. It is remembered as a big event in the life of the Party organization."[28] "The speech [of Brezhnev at the plenum of the Central Committee in November 1981] showed the big . . . work performed after the 26th

[23]A. Litovchenko, *P,* July 27, 1981.

[24]Editorial, *P,* April 10, 1982.

[25]G. Mikhailov, *PZh,* 1975, No. 11, p. 50.

[26]L. Gorshkov, *K,* 1976, No. 1, p. 14.

[27]K. Chorenko, *K,* 1981, No. 13, p. 14.

[28]F. Loshchenko, *K,* 1970, No. 1, p. 26.

Congress of the CPSU, noted the increased activeness of the masses in work and in politics."[29]

Every required conduct will heighten the activeness of those engaged in it as well as of those affected by it; this consequence may be one of its major, and not always manifest, objectives. Thus provisions should be made "so that *the study of Marxist-Leninist theory* . . . fosters the further growth of . . . activeness in work. . . . "[30] "Unfolding *criticism and self-criticism,* the City Committee and the primary Party organizations . . . strive to heighten the activeness of the communists. . . . "[31] "The *exchange of Party documents* . . . was utilized for the further activation of intra-Party life. . . . "[32] "*The preparation of the coming [Party] Congress* is a powerful lever for heightening the . . . activeness of both communists and non-Party people."[33]

* * * * * * *

The Kremlin's insistence that communists "are obliged to show high activeness day after day"[34] and heighten the activeness of everybody else is, I would guess, a reaction to its belief that human beings, if left to themselves, are apt to show low and declining activeness—while that attribute needs to be high and rising to achieve success or even merely to avert disaster.

Where cadres seem, when observed at a distance, to be usefully busy, they may turn out to be nonproductive when the observer "penetrates deeply" into their doings. "Externally some managers conduct themselves faultlessly"; yet "they do not show any results."[35] A close look will show why:

> Take, for instance, the Party organization in the *Glavpromstroi* of Krasnodar. . . . On first sight everything goes well: Party meetings are conducted regularly as well as sessions of the bureau, plans of measures are being composed in precise fashion, protocols correctly signed. However, an analysis conducted by the Party territory committee . . . showed that the discussion of questions at meetings and in the bureau often shows a formal character, the decisions adopted are not concrete, there is no *kontrol'* over fulfillment. The Party organization does not really influence the work of the [economic] apparatus. . . .[36]

---

[29]Editorial, *P,* November 21, 1981.

[30]A. Kovalenko, *K,* 1978, No. 14, p. 30. Emphasis added.

[31]P. Kudryavtsev, *PZh,* 1975, No. 21, p. 25. Emphasis added.

[32]A. Rybakov, *K,* 1974, No. 10, p. 51. Emphasis added.

[33]L. Brezhnev, at the Central Committee plenum, June 23, 1980, Brezhnev 1981, p. 366. Emphasis added.

[34]G. Mikhailov, *PZh,* 1975, No. 11, p. 52.

[35]V. Makarenko, *PZh,* 1979, No. 23, p. 48.

> Every time we analyze the discipline in implementation of particular workers . . . such an analysis helps one to understand much. It happens that after it one looks at a person with completely different eyes. Let us take the former second secretary of the Party committee in the city of Borisov, V. Kapultsevich. The province committee of Minsk entertained not a bad opinion of him. But after close acquaintance with the acts of this person we understood something different. Kapultsevich knew how to speak well but did not put into effect a practical, everyday leadership of the primary Party organizations. . . .[37]

With "an appearance of . . . strenuous activity," numerous components of management "whirl around in idling fashion":

> The office and the waiting room of A. I. Ereva is always full of people. Some with a report, some for a mission, and some simply to express their regard. If you look at it from the side, all are busy, all are in movement and hence working. But this is only an appearance.[38]

If this is not "eyewash," it is because these cadres deceive themselves to some extent before they mislead others by their "show of activeness," "a show of fulfilling missions (*pokaznaya ispolnitel'nost'*) behind which often . . . inaction hides."[39] "They adopt measures only for the sake of appearance."[40]

The result of their busyness is the same as if they had not acted at all: "an activeness for show, and inaction in fact."[41] Merely avoiding this may be counted as an excellence. Of a cadre one may note with appreciation that "he does not run in place."[42]

When cadres do act with some effect, they may still be only responding to external pressures rather than originating their actions. "There are still many managers who work, as it is put in a letter received by us, on the principle: 'they pushed us and we fell, they picked us up and we proceeded'"—while "what is needed is continuous initiative—initiative always and in all things."[44] "A communist does

[36]S. Medunov, *PZh,* 1979, No. 12, p. 16.

[37]V. Nikulich, *P,* February 9, 1982.

[38]P. Masherov, *P,* June 15, 1980.

[39]Editorial, *PZh,* 1983, No. 7, p. 9.

[40]K. Bondarenko, *P,* September 3, 1980.

[41]Editorial, *K,* 1971, No. 10, p. 12.

[42]Editorial, *P,* November 29, 1980.

[43]Editorial, *P,* November 29, 1980.

[44]L. Brezhnev, 26th Party Congress, March 3, 1981, Brezhnev 1981a, p. 734.

not wait for prompting as to how to behave. . . . "[45] (In such a context it is, of course, not mentioned that acting without orders may be called by a negative name and punished.)

Then there are those who, while effective to a degree, yet "do not utilize all their possibilities for the development of production."[46] "Some comrades relate to their mission listlessly, and enjoy that."[47] For instance, "sometimes ministries . . . approve advanced initiatives in merely a formal fashion, [and] do not work in a persevering and consequential manner for their realization."[48] Even for "specialists" in production-related R&D, it may be declared "inadmissible" that they work "in idling fashion."[49] "It happens that somebody arrives at work in time, leaves at the proper time, is not late back after lunch, but works weakly or is entirely inactive. . . . "[50]

In the pervasive Bolshevik mode of refusing to recognize events in the middle of a range between nothing and all, and sensing them as essentially nothing (as already noted), low performers may be viewed as nonperformers, as "those who do not work, but are merely present in their place of work."[51] Recalling how he had refused a middle level of activity in his earlier life, Brezhnev asks, "Could I require . . . high effort of others if I myself was slacking off?"[52] "Of the lack of initiative," one may recall, "V. I. Lenin said that it is a hidden form of inaction."[53]

Any difficulty may become a pretext for yielding to the urge not to act. "When replacement parts [of a machine] are missing, don't sit there without work. . . . "[54]

One may find inaction where one surely did not expect it. "The director . . . had cut himself off from the collective. 'But this is a person given to inaction [*bezdel'nik*]!' those conducting the verification said, astonished."[55]

On the other hand, "engaging in inaction [*bezdeistvovat'*]" may also be expected as often as it is rejected. "And now," one may say in depicting an "autocratic" cadre, "began the scolding. . . ." For what?

---

[45]Editorial, *P*, April 7, 1983.

[46]L. Brezhnev, quoted in F. Morgun, *PZh*, 1979, No. 12, p. 23.

[47]A. Girenko, *PZh*, 1980, No. 22, p. 16.

[48]Editorial, *P*, May 30, 1980.

[49]Editorial, *P*, November 28, 1981.

[50]V. Kuzmishchev, *P*, March 23, 1983.

[51]V. Loginov, *P*, March 20, 1980.

[52]L. Brezhnev 1981b, p. 20.

[53]I. Edneral, *P*, June 6, 1980.

[54]V. Nasonova, *PZh*, 1973, No. 4, p. 48.

[55]Yu. Makhrin, *P*, January 18, 1982.

"Inaction."[56] Sometimes the [Party] Commission . . . questioning [managers] . . . spent a significant part of its effort and time on the collection of various kinds of little facts by which one could 'indisputably' prove *the inaction* . . . of economic managers."[57]

Then action—or, rather, the pretense of it to oneself and/or others—may become a means of invalidating an always plausible charge of inaction: "Everybody can see: we are not sitting with hands folded."[58]

It is, of course, not in the Kremlin's interest to dwell upon its own contribution to the penchant for doing nothing: making subordinates "prefer to an independent decision the 'faultlessness' of doing nothing."[59] It is rather suggested that what is involved is the displeasure of doing, perhaps combined with the pleasure of merely looking: "the position of passively gazing on events unfolding by themselves,"[60] becoming "simple recorders of events."[61]

One may, having exerted oneself at first, cease action, predicting that success is now assured. Then is manifested, for instance, "our inclination to rely on the 'movement by itself'" (*samodvizhenie*) of a collective initiative.[62] "To some comrades the first bread [obtained from the Virgin Lands] seemed already the end of all of our work."[63] But, the Kremlin objects, "it would be radically wrong to believe that . . . tasks . . . can be solved by leaving them to themselves."[64] It is more likely that "the main work is still ahead."[65] "We rejoice that Magnitka [the metallurgical *kombinat* at Magnitogorsk] has begun the 11th Five-Year Plan well. But before us is still an enormous amount of work. . . . "[66]

The penchant for inaction may prove overwhelming at the very moment of crisis. "In the life and work of a communist, sharp situations occur. How should one act? One may be tempted to sit it out where it is quiet, to become an observer from the sidelines in the conflict."[67]

---

[56] F. Robinov, *K,* 1975, No. 11, p. 61.

[57] A. Gudkov, *P,* January 18, 1980. Emphasis added.

[58] K. Bondarenko, *P,* September 3, 1980.

[59] A. Chernyak, *PZh,* 1980, No. 19, p. 11.

[60] Editorial, *K,* 1980, No. 9, p. 7.

[61] Zh. Chesnokov, *P,* January 29, 1980.

[62] N. Kirichenko, *P,* May 26, 1980.

[63] L. Brezhnev, *Tselina,* Brezhnev 1979, p. 168.

[64] L. Brezhnev, quoted in *PZh,* 1977, No. 6, p. 28.

[65] Editorial, *P,* July 27, 1981.

[66] A. Litovchenko, *P,* July 17, 1981.

[67] V. Liventsov, *P,* June 17, 1980.

"There are Party members"—even more so, non-Party people—"who, when encountering defects, behave as if they had noticed nothing."[68] "One milkmaid, member of the district committee of the Party, saw that feed was being wasted, but did not in timely fashion sound the alarm."[69] "Sometimes the equipment is inactive. Some... managers . . . see this, yet take no measures";[70] or they may "passively observe a worker turning out defective products."[71] "Instead of proceeding severely against those guilty of failure in the task [of producing the advanced tractor *Bogatyr*], instead of adopting decisive measures for the improvement of the operation, the leaders of the Ministry of Agricultural Machinebuilding and the industrial Associations connected with it, year after year, merely observe defects and lagging behind."[72]

Such inaction may be accompanied by "the hope that everything will come out all right by itself"[73]—to which the Party top opposes the presumption (already noted) that an affair left to itself will rather go from bad to worse. Against "the habit of waiting and hoping for an 'off chance,'"[74] the leadership demands "don't wait, act."[75]

Inaction, the leadership knows, may also be justified by the expectation that somebody else will do the job: "If we do not deliver the cotton-picking machines we are producing on time, nobody is going to do it for us."[76]

Or one may underestimate one's capacities. "This is too much," people will say, "this is beyond our capabilities"—an excuse that shows "how far passivity may lead."[77] Many disruptions are explained by the fact that "comrades . . . lowered their arms, expressing their powerlessness."[78] "Everyone to whom one turns for help merely spreads out his arms"[79]—a reaction so tempting that it seems appropriate to disallow it

---

[68]Editorial, *PZh*, 1978, No. 13, p. 7.

[69]G. Kondryukov, *PZh*, 1978, No. 17, p. 34.

[70]V. Makarenko,*PZh*, 1979, No. 23, p. 44.

[71]*K*, 1981, No. 3, p. 12.

[72]I. Totskii, *P*, January 7, 1982.

[73]Editorial, *K*, 1982, No. 2, p. 8.

[74]V. Gerasimov and A. Zolin, *P*, May 6, 1982.

[75]Headline, *P*, April 4, 1983.

[76]E. Mamatkulov, *P*, April 29, 1983.

[77]L. Brezhnev, *Tselina*, Brezhnev 1979, p. 170.

[78]A. Korolev, quoted by A. Chernyak, *P*, November 29, 1982.

[79]V. Bykovskii, *PZh*, 1972, No. 3, p. 35.

explicitly: "A communist is obliged not to spread his arms helplessly in the face of difficulties. . . . "[80]

Nor ought he then to allege, or even to believe, that a manageable job is infeasible because of "all sorts of 'objective' causes,"[81] an excuse particularly irritating to the leadership, which sees its own vocabulary used against it.

Beyond the helpless spreading of one's arms, there is the "indifferent . . . waving" of them. "There are enterprises in which . . . modernization proceeds slowly; the rules of economy and conservation are not followed. Hence, plans are not fulfilled, premiums [are] not paid. . . . The simplest reaction is . . . to shrug it off."[82] People are apt to gaze "indifferently [i.e., with equanimity, without participation—NL] on defects."[83] There are "communists who, encountering negative events, appear not to be concerned."[84] "It seems that nothing concerns him. . . . Around him there is inefficiency, but he passes that by."[85] "The situation has deteriorated in a number of farms in the province of Kiev which even recently were advanced. . . . This has occurred before the eyes of the Ministry of Sovkhozes . . ., [of] the district and city committees, and of the Kiev province committee of the Party." Yet "being indifferent while the situation in the collectives is deteriorating" is "impermissible."[86] Indeed, it seems appropriate to express "nonindifference (*neravnodushie*) to all that happens."[87] The absence of indifference may thus become a mark of excellence: "There were no indifferent ones."[88] "An unindifferent person: thus I would describe the essence of this communist. Unindifferent to all that happens around him, even if it does not concern him at first sight. . . . A communist, that is, an unindifferent person. . . . "[89] "The true Party leader has nonindifference."[90] "A communist is concerned with everything."[91] His is "an ardent interestedness."[92]

---

[80]V. Grishin, *PZh,* 1972, No. 1, p. 15.

[81]Editorial note, *P,* January 16, 1983.

[82]Ibid.

[83]A. Yarofarov, *P,* August 15, 1980.

[84]A. Pelshe, *K,* 1971, No. 11, p. 29.

[85]V. Kozhenyako, *PZh,* 1979, No. 20, p. 26.

[86]V. Shcherbitskii, speech, November 25, 1981, *Pravda Ukrainy,* November 26, FBIS, December 21, p. R-16.

[87]Unsigned article, *K,* 1981, No. 3, p. 9.

[88]K. Khartsev, *PZh,* 1978, No. 16, p. 66.

[89]E. Klimchenko, *P,* April 11, 1982.

[90]I. Kapitonov, *K,* 1982, No. 7, p. 14.

[91]F. Kozyrev, *PZh,* 1972, No. 3, p. 49.

[92]A. Chernyak, *P,* June 3, 1982.

To draw people out of their indifference is hard, requiring some mastery: "The discoveries . . . and conclusions . . . of Lenin left nobody indifferent."[93]

Just as indifference is likely to be accompanied by a sense of one's incapacity to affect one's environment, nonindifference implies a rejection of this belief, a sense of power over events. "We again and again convince ourselves"—so strong is the stance to be rejected—"that a Party worker is worthy of his name when he is capable of influencing current processes. . . . "[94] "We communists do not have the right"—but perhaps we have the urge—"to exist as prisoners of circumstances, without will and without aim, to depend on how things turn out."[95] It is precisely the "art" of communists "to influence events";[96] theirs is "the striving not to trail along at the back, but to subjugate circumstances, to direct events. . . . "[97]

"An efficient (*delovityi*) person, as a rule, finds a way out from the most difficult situation";[98] *delovitost'* is a Party quality.

So is an eye for the "reserves" likely to be hidden in a given situation, which may thus offer possibilities larger than those the ordinary person perceives. Upon discovering them, in one such case, "many workers of the enterprise marveled: 'How much depends on ourselves!'"[99]

The urge toward inaction and hence the fight for *aktivnost'* never end. Observing that "literally before our eyes the world is changing" and thereby perhaps inviting the temptation just to sit and look, Brezhnev at a Party Congress protests that "our Party is not a passive spectator of these changes. No, we are active participants in them."[100]

Nothing can be won except by fighting with all available means. "That remarkable commander of Soviet industry, Ivan Alekseevich Likhachev, loved the word *drat'sya* [knocking about]. He often declared, 'One must *drat'sya* for our norms, our deadlines, our accounts, our money.'"[101]

---

[93]V. Zagladin, *K,* 1980, No. 3, p. 28.

[94]G. Bandrovskii, *PZh,* 1980, No. 17, p. 43.

[95]V. Vinogradov, *P,* March 24, 1980.

[96]K. Chernenko 1978, p. 21.

[97]V. Shcherbitskii 1978, p. 132.

[98]V. Murakhovskii, quoted by A. Chernyak, *P,* December 1, 1981.

[99]K. Lebedev, *P,* August 4, 1980.

[100]L. Brezhnev, speech at the 25th Party Congress, February 24, 1976, Brezhnev 1976, p. 450.

[101]M. Krukov, *P,* April 18, 1982.

Specifically, activeness has an "attacking" character, and "attack presupposes activeness . . . the striving to move forward."[102]

Doing that, we are surely not sagging, *not decreasing* our activeness—a propensity as much feared by the Party top as that of limiting oneself to a low level of activeness to start with. "What began like a stormy mountain stream gradually becomes shallow."[103] "He started work with fire. But then he cooled off."[104] "Having proclaimed the new initiative, they gradually cooled toward it"[105]—something that is only to be expected: "An initiative that is condemned to take its own course runs to seed and dies."[106] "A collective is passionately concerned with work discipline, arranges for a campaign in favor of economizing resources. But then the campaign disappears. What has begun does not become an everyday affair."[107] Often the Central Committee had to "observe that some territory, province, city, and district Party committees weakened *kontrol'*."[108] The top level may then go to the length of pointing out that "those Party committees act correctly who . . . do *not* weaken efforts."[109] If "things are left to themselves," many a manager might become "the person who . . . gradually cuts himself off from the Party organization, becomes indifferent and passive . . . transforms himself into an . . . ordinary mediocrity (*obyvatel'*)."[110]

High activeness is likely to bring success—but success is likely to breed a decline in what brought it. Human beings are inclined to rest on laurels: to bask in a satisfactory state, to become complacent, to grow content with what they have achieved, to lose dissatisfaction with what they have attained. Hence, they are apt to overlook the fact that it takes as much activeness to preserve as to gain. "This quality," one will say about a prized person, "is formed in a person not at once and not for always . . . it can be lost."[111] Indeed, it will be lost if one does not struggle as hard to maintain it as one fought to acquire it. "One must consolidate such a direction of events," one may say about a

---

[102]L. Brezhnev, speech, April 23, 1974, Brezhnev 1976, p. 53.

[103]N. Kirichenko, *P,* May 26, 1980.

[104]A. Popernyak, *P,* September 11, 1981.

[105]A. Margovenko, *P,* March 5, 1982.

[106]K. Chernenko, *Voprosy Istorii KPSS,* 1982, No. 2, pp. 3–19.

[107]M. Krukov, *P,* January 29, 1983.

[108]K. Chernenko 1978, p. 68.

[109]Editorial, *PZh,* 1980, No. 16, p. 11. Emphasis added.

[110]F. Kozyrev, *PZh,* 1972, No. 3, pp. 50–51.

[111]V. Shcherbitskii, *PZh,* 1981, No. 15, p. 13.

favorable development, "one must fight for it. Otherwise, everything may roll down the incline backward."[112] Thus "Party organizations constantly fight against . . . complacency."[113]

They have many targets. "We have, as it were, stopped," a foreman reports about his factory, "for we are prosperous."[114] "The section of foreman Comrade Mishin in Workshop 21 worked well. Then the leader became complacent, weakened in his efforts to educate the collective, stopped being interested in the needs and demands of his subordinates. As a result, the section's indicators fell sharply."[115] "This still often happens: A person has attained high results—and then he becomes complacent. He goes, as one says, along a well-trodden groove. He works in an old-fashioned manner; he moves not by creative search, but by inertia. Inertia, as is well known, pushes forward for a time. But then movement slows up until it dies down."[116]

* * * * * * * *

It is up to the Party to prevent such an outcome by "aim-directed work for the elimination of inertia . . .,"[117] as with the dispelling of any other form of inaction. If "contemporary revisionists . . . strive to render the working class . . . leaderless, to leave it without . . . a leader and organizer," it is so as "to condemn it to doing nothing [*bezdeistvie*]."[118] Counteracting the propensity toward inaction, the Party is vigilant to prevent the catastrophe that would otherwise ensue. "Utilizing a variety of . . . methods for heightening the activity of communists, the Party organization of the city bases itself on the decision of the 24th Congress of the CPSU: the Party does not accept passivity. . . . "[119]

Always, as Brezhnev asserted about the reconstruction of the steel plant at Zaporozhe after the War, "it was important *not to lose speed,* to take fortress after fortress as at the front."[120] So far from losing, one should *gather speed.* Eternal acceleration is the most satisfying, but also the only fully reassuring, posture: "not reducing but accelerating the tempi of production."[121]

---

[112]L. Brezhnev, speech, April 26, 1979, Brezhnev 1981a, p. 33.

[113]F. Morgun, *PZh,* 1979, No. 12, p. 23.

[114]K. Bondarenko, *P,* September 3, 1980.

[115]T. Gureev, *PZh,* 1973, No. 15, p. 55.

[116]S. Marasulov, *P,* November 24, 1981.

[117]Ibid.

[118]V. Grishin, *K,* 1979, No. 7, pp. 21–22.

[119]E. Podshchipkov, *PZh,* 1973, No. 7, p. 50.

[120]L. Brezhnev, *Vorozhdenie,* Brezhnev 1979, p. 67. Emphasis added.

[121]Editorial, *P,* May 15, 1980.

Although everybody ought to demand of *himself* the high activeness required for such a result, the "exactingness" of *others* toward oneself is in fact indispensable: a service that only others can and must render me, and I them. While "an atmosphere of nonexactingness toward oneself and others necessarily begets inaction,"[122] a "mutual exactingness of one toward the other"[123] is both necessary and sufficient to prevent that disaster. "All the workers of the workshop came to see Stakhanov: let us establish a common obligation [in socialist competition] and we shall exercise surveillance over (*kontrolirovat'*) each other. . . . "[124] "I could adduce many examples where the timely intervention and help of Party organizations, committees, [or] comrades helped a person to free himself from passivity, of the wish to serve time on the side."[125] "Mutual exactingness . . . engenders the desire to work creatively, with initiative. And, inversely, leniency softens people, leads to passiveness."[126] "Lack of exactingness toward oneself and others . . . inevitably engenders inaction."[127]

"Exactingness" toward the other thus being essential, one must not be content with merely keeping it up—next, it would fall—but must encourage it to rise constantly—"the constant heightening of exactingness toward the cadres"[128] —preferably at a rising rate.

Any Party operation (as already implied) may (indeed, is apt to) aim at *raising* activeness. "Criticism and self-criticism are the necessary conditions for a rise in the activeness of communists."[129] "The realization by the Party of measures favoring the further development of intra-Party democracy activates the communists even more."[130] "A communist has the right to know what has happened to his proposal [made, for instance, at a primary Party meeting]. Being informed about this develops his activeness. . . . "[131] "The whole work concerning the renewal of Party cards is raising the activeness of every communist. We have to deal with every communist manifesting passivity, to discover the causes of the passivity, to work out measures directed

---

[122]A. Stakhanov, *P,* January 3, 1982.

[123]Editorial, *P,* January 21, 1982.

[124]A. Speranskii, *P,* July 4, 1981.

[125]V. Sapega, *P,* December 12, 1982.

[126]Editorial, *P,* January 21, 1982.

[127]N. Lisenkov, *P,* August 6, 1982.

[128]K. Chernenko 1980, p. 216.

[129]P. Shelest, *K,* 1971, No. 12, p. 28.

[130]Loc. cit., p. 26.

[131]Editorial, *P,* January 6, 1982.

toward the removal of these causes."[132] "Party meetings are destined to foster the rise of the activeness of all communists. . . . The Party committees conducted many meetings in which everything was done that was necessary to . . . further raise the activeness of the communists. Many other measures were realized, so as to foster a rise in the activeness of the communists."[133]

With a variety of means for raising activeness available to Party bodies, in every situation the question should be posed and answered, "which forms of . . . work must be applied so as to raise even further the activeness of communists and non-Party people in work and in society . . . ?"[134] An article may be entitled "An Important Means for the Heightening of Activeness,"[135] or "A Powerful Tool for Heightening the Activeness of the Masses."[136]

Beneath the very top, every level and variety of "worker" within the Party and outside it is likely to be the target of attempts by others to lift his activeness. To be sure, "the work activeness of *the workers* is directly proportional to the activeness of the communists,"[137] who are operating on the workers to enhance their activeness or to keep it from falling. "The decisions of the 25th Congress require that all Party committees stimulate *government and economic organs, social organizations*, and work collectives to be more active."[138] "The District Committee has created a school of Party-building where *members of the Committee, secretaries of Party organizations, members of Party committees and of bureaus of Party organizations, and other activists* study. . . . Studying has permitted the raising of the activeness of *members of all elected organs.*"[139] "The Party committee and the Party bureau of the *kolkhoz* and *sovkhos* activate *the agitators and political information specialists.*"[140] "All this . . . fostered the activation of *scientific-research work in the domain of Party-building*":[141] the specialists in activating need to be activated themselves.

To "activate" is not only every Party body's task, it may be its dominant objective. "To activate the masses of communists by all means is

---

[132]V. Marisov, *PZh*, 1972, No. 16, p. 34.

[133]F. Loshchenko, *K*, 1970, No. 1, p. 23.

[134]G. Krivoshein, *K*, 1971, No. 18, p. 33.

[135]V. Smirnov, *PZh*, 1972, No. 2, p. 43.

[136]*PZh*, 1976, No. 1, p. 23.

[137]E. Smolkin, *PZh*, 1975, No. 21, p. 61. Emphasis added.

[138]I. Kapitonov, *K*, 1976, No. 11, p. 34. Emphasis added.

[139]I. Senkin, *K*, 1971, No. 1, p. 27.

[140]V. Ilyin, *PZh*, 1975, No. 13, p. 19. Emphasis added.

[141]Unsigned article, *PZh*, 1975, No. 3, p. 16. Emphasis added.

the most important task of today."[142] "The *chief* task of the communists is to make the work activeness of Soviet people continue to rise."[143] "Continuous concern for the unswerving rise of the . . . activeness of the masses remains the most important content of Party work."[144] "The question [was]," one reads about an important moment in the life of a primary organization, "whom one could now charge with leadership in the Party organization, who could *raise the activeness* of the communists in this enterprise."[145] As "all Party organizations have one common task, the activation of the Party mass," the "most important form of life within the Party is the Party meeting"; for "if well-prepared and skillfully conducted, it activates the masses of communists. . . . "[146]

One is influenced, to be sure, by one's peers. "It is said correctly: the communist is active when the Party organization itself is active."[147] Yet one's entire group is mainly "activated" by what is above one; as one "activates" what is below one.

While it may be surmised that in the secret view the Party top should activate *all* levels beneath it, including the Central Committees of the Republics, all that is readily declared is that "the Central Committee strives to maximally activate the primary Party organizations, the workshop Party organizations, and the [lowest] Party groups."[148]

But without such consideration for those directly beneath him, a First Secretary of a Province Committee can state, "our obligation [is] to secure high activeness of the Party organizations."[149] Of course, "the primary Party organizations must . . . activize the [yet lower] Party organizations of the workshops and the Party groups."[150]

The objective of all these endeavors from above, whether targeted on the next lower level or jumping over it, is, to be sure, the "Party mass," which in turn has to activate the "[non-Party] masses." Thus, "Party committees . . . are charged with securing the growth of the work activity of the masses."[151] Correspondingly, according to a First Secretary of a Province Committee, "the Party organizations of the province

---

[142]V. Vonskikh, *PZh,* 1976, No. 16, p. 39. Emphasis added.

[143]Sh. Siyakhakov, *PZh,* 1976, No. 23, p. 65. Emphasis added.

[144]K. Chernenko 1980, p. 396.

[145]G. Kalugin, *PZh,* 1972, No. 14, p. 45. Emphasis added.

[146]N. Polozov, *PZh,* 1970, No. 7, p. 41.

[147]R. Stakheev, *P,* March 30, 1982.

[148]L. Brezhnev, speech at the 26th Party Congress, February 23, 1981, Brezhnev 1981a, p. 717.

[149]V. Vorotnikov, *PZh,* 1975, No. 14, p. 17.

[150]Editorial, *PZh,* 1972, No. 18, p. 6.

[151]Unsigned article, *PZh,* 1976, No. 12, p. 23.

aim all their work at developing a surge of the work activity of the workers, kolkhoz members, intelligentsia. . . . "[152]

While the Party top, I surmise, takes it for granted that activeness spreads from above—ultimately from that unmoved mover, "the Central Committee"—toward below, it thinly veils this truth by declarations about the "inexhaustible energy," not of itself but of "the masses," about "activeness . . . issuing 'from below' . . . from the very depths of society. . . . "[153] (The need for quotation marks around "from below" is the justification for including the entire sentence.) Whereas, in this vein, "the energy of the people" is "boiling" by itself,[154] it is in the Party top's usually secret belief the Party that "develops the . . . energy of the masses"[155] —not only by disinhibiting it and diverting it from its unproductive and self-damaging "spontaneous" directions to efficient ones, but even by instilling energy into the masses (from what fund is modestly not indicated). A primary Party organization will normally "confer on all workers of the factory a charge of new energy."[156] "In all towns and villages of the country the November plenum of the Central Committee of the CPSU . . . called forth an influx of energy,"[157] as allegedly does every plenum, indeed every major public act occurring at the Party's top. This formula merely expands, I suspect, upon a belief at upper Party levels that endowment with activeness varies directly with one's level in the hierarchy, where the Central Committee is at the top and the masses are at the bottom.

The higher the activeness of a given level, the higher that of the level below. "The Party groups began to act in a more active fashion, and their influence on the activity of their collectives grew."[158]

If activeness at a certain level is inadequate, look for the same deficiency at higher levels (a chain that is, however, not pursued beyond the middle levels). "The kolkhoz in the name of Zhdanov in the district of Shargorod [Ukraine] was one of middle performance. It was considered [higher up] that its land was worse than that of others. Hence, particular demands were not made on its managers. This led to the chairman and then the specialists and managers of the middle level working without straining themselves, losing initiative, reconciling

---

[152]V. Vorotnikov, *PZh,* 1975, No. 14, p. 17.

[153]Editorial, *K,* 1978, No. 14, p. 14.

[154]Unsigned article, *PZh,* 1977, No. 10, p. 3.

[155]I. Kapitonov, *K,* 1981, No. 9, p. 13.

[156]A. Kurshakova, *PZh,* 1980, No. 4, p. 38.

[157]Editorial, *K,* 1978, No. 18, p. 14.

[158]A. Tsarkov, *PZh,* 1972, No. 4, p. 54.

themselves to low indicators. The kolkhoz began to lag."[159] "Some Party committees penetrate only shallowly into the work of the organs of People's Control. . . . Such conduct has a negative effect on the activity of People's Controllers."[160] "Not a few commissions [Party commissions for the *kontrol'* of management] are inactive. Why? Sometimes they are left to themselves. The Party committees and the bureau do not direct their work, are not interested in their plans, do not render them . . . support."[161]

> A contrast between a high performance in producing a chemical factory and a low performance in producing residential housing: "In the first case, Party organizations concentrated their attention on the . . . object, putting into action the many . . . methods of influence at their disposal. Workers' relays, support given to innovators and instructors, the education of people in the best traditions, the consideration of questions in meetings of the staff and of the bureau of the Province Committee—all of these means were employed. This showed in the results.
>
> "In the other case, the builders of residential housing were left to themselves. Defects in work, violations of work discipline did not bother anybody [in the Party] particularly. Hence, houses with serious defects were built."[162]

The negative event "comes by itself"; the positive one has to be forced into existence, strenuously and precariously.

SURGE (*POD'EM*)

Just *how* does the Party pretend to activate economic personnel, from unskilled workers to directors, without substituting itself (the more "active" ones) for them (the less "active" ones), which it denies doing?

Well, in one mode, by inducing them (the less active ones) to become more like ourselves with our higher activeness. Just as "there are . . . sometimes those who introduce elements of inertness and passivity into the collective,"[163] there are always those whose high activeness is infectious: the "personal example set by communists"—a major point needing no illustration.

---

[159] V. Taratuta, *PZh*, 1976, No. 22, pp. 10–11.

[160] Editorial, *P*, February 19, 1980.

[161] Editorial, *P*, July 31, 1980.

[162] A. Vorotnikov, *P*, May 22, 1980.

[163] L. Brezhnev, speech, April 3, 1974, Brezhnev 1976, p. 28.

In a second mode—and this merits elaboration—the Party apparatus pretends to induce *elation* in its "lowest links"—in the "Party mass" and "the masses"—and thereby to increase the amount of work furnished as well as the productivity.

To be sure, the Bolshevik's conduct should not be affected by "mood." The Party's top level may publicly express its contempt (and, obscurely, its fear) for a reaction that is "a mood and not a conviction, doubts and mutterings instead of a sober analysis of the facts. . . . "[164] But a Bolshevik must also never forget that the performance of the masses depends precisely on feelings. "There exists . . . a direct connection between mood and work."[165] "A good mood," one may insist, "is not a minor matter, but an important reserve of production."[166] "In what mood do you go to work? If a collective awaits you at work which is . . . [here the present reader should supply the required characteristics—NL], one can say with assurance: your mood is good. And because this is so, you will be highly productive."[167] "When a person is in a good mood, he works better. Indicators of production depend directly on the mood of each of us."[168] "In the accounting-electoral Party meetings in the Leningrad Association Svetlana, the main theme of many was that reserves of growth are located not only in the perfecting of technology and organization. No less are they contained . . . in the mood of people."[169] "The secretary of the Party organization of the factory, Aleksandr Andreevich Golovin, is often asked: What is the 'secret' of the successes of your collective? He always answers: 'Its high work mood (*trudovoi nastroi*).'"[170]

The connection between mood and work may be taken for granted. One may then say: ". . . mood *and hence* the quality of work,"[171] "the mood in the work collective *and hence also* the indicators of production."[172] On a recent New Year's Day "L. Brezhnev . . . wished [the Soviet people] a good mood, success in work. . . . "[173] "The mood, the tonus in work (*tvorcheskii tonus*) of people. . . . "[174]

---

[164]A. Pelshe, *K,* 1980, No. 2, p. 31.

[165]N. Voitsuk, *PZh,* 1978, No. 21, p. 73.

[166]An unsigned article, *PZh,* 1973, No. 16, p. 67.

[167]Editorial, *P,* October 27, 1982.

[168]A manager, quoted in V. Ivanov, *P,* January 22, 1980.

[169]Editorial, *P,* October 27, 1982.

[170]V. Stepanov, *PZh,* 1972, No. 18, p. 62.

[171]V. Kalinin, *PZh,* 1979, No. 16, p. 63. Emphasis added.

[172]L. Brezhnev, at the Central Committee Plenum, November 1981, quoted in I. Vasilyev, *P,* November 19, 1981. Emphasis added.

[173]Editorial, *P,* January 2, 1981.

[174]Editorial, *P,* November 25, 1981.

"The time has come," an editorial writer points out, "to supplement the inspiration of the struggle for a high speed of production, born in the first Five-Year Plan, with the inspiration of the struggle for high effectiveness and quality of work. This must become the chief inspiration in building the economy";[175] that there can be no high economic performance without "inspiration" is self-evident.

Having performance in mind, one may merely mention mood: "And a Good Mood Prevails," declares a headline.[176]

Mood is a delicate thing, sharply sensitive to many factors. When discussing "the economics of quality," one may observe that "well-done products raise mood."[177] On the other hand, a case shows how "one person [a senior engineer] makes people nervous and spoils their mood. . . ."[178]

Fortunately, the Party is master over mood and thereby over performance at work. First of all, it determines conditions of life and work. "The conditions of daily life," so runs a typical enunciation of the obvious, "influence the mood of workers, their ability to work." Improving these conditions is to "raise the mood of the masses for work."[179] In a workshop, windows were washed after not having been cleaned for a long time: "The very day on which it got lighter in the workshop the productivity of work rose by 10 percent. Imagine! Many were astonished, but there is no secret—simply, the mood of people rose."[180]

But there is also the Party's "organizational," "educational," and "ideological" impact on workers—an impact that the Party's top, with whatever degree of sincerity, presents as powerful. "The primary Party organizations . . . inspire the workers . . . and, as the people rightly say, being inspired is the mother of success."[181] "The Party secretaries know how to . . . lift the mood of people and their working activeness."[182] "The development of the production of motors confirms . . . this truth: where Party organizations . . . undertake educational and organizational work among the workers . . . there will be a

---

[175]Editorial, *K,* 1980, No. 9, p. 6.

[176]*P,* October 3, 1980.

[177]Editorial, *P,* February 11, 1982.

[178]L. Gorbachev, *PZh,* 1979, No. 17, p. 76.

[179]Editorial, *P,* August 2, 1981.

[180]G. Kononov, *P,* June 18, 1982.

[181]P. Shelest, *K,* 1971, No. 12, p. 16.

[182]V. Dolgikh, *PZh,* 1979, No. 13, p. 40.

surge (*pod'em*) and great practical results will be obtained."[183] "The communists were able to create in the work collective a mood in which all members struggled with extreme activeness for . . . the utilization of every working minute."[184] "Thoroughly knowing . . . the human soul, Kovalev [a Party cadre] is able to affect the mood of the collective; and the effect of this is sometimes greater than that from a technical reconstruction."[185]

Again, when the Party's mastery over moods is affirmed, the connection between mood and performance may be taken for granted. Arguing that "it is possible . . . to *obtain* enthusiasm in work . . . every day"—while, it is understood, a spontaneous high is a passing thing—one may conclude that "because this is so, it is possible to furnish a high product every day."[186] "The Province Committee strove to create . . . an atmosphere that would lift the mood and the energy of the communists. . . . "[187] "The work of Party organizations . . . is reflected in the mood of people, their relationship to the work at hand."[188] "How did he," one may ask about a model manager, "win fame? First of all, by his ability to utilize . . . people's reserves of good mood."[189] "Creating a Good Mood" is made the title of an article,[190] which is, of course, interested in conduct rather than soul, in performance rather than feeling.

It thus becomes a major defect for a Party cadre to be "indifferent" and hence "inattentive" to moods of subordinates. "Some leaders consider that . . . emotions do not concern them."[191] "We . . . did not always penetrate deeply into the moods of people"[192]—a failing characteristic of economic managers. There are, of course, exceptions:

> During the last years many economic managers have increased their ability to combine administrative work with the education of people. There are not a few examples where a commander of production . . . is, in the full meaning of the word, the soul of the collective. . . . In the Valuisk District of Belgorod Province . . . in the buttermilk *kombinat* . . . the greatest contribution to educational work, as all communists admit, is made by the director of the

[183] A. Kirilenko, *K,* 1978, No. 7, p. 25.

[184] G. Mikhailov, *PZh,* 1975, No. 11, p. 50.

[185] V. Poltoratskii, *K,* 1974, No. 18, p. 53.

[186] V. Oderov, *K,* 1973, No. 4, pp. 76–77. Emphasis added.

[187] I. Senkin, *K,* 1971, No. 1, p. 24.

[188] K. Muraviev, *P,* April 15, 1981.

[189] Editorial, *P,* July 24, 1980.

[190] *PZh,* No. 16, p. 66.

[191] Editorial, *P,* December 29, 1981.

[192] G. Krivoshein, *PZh,* 1979, No. 16, p. 40.

> enterprise, Sergei Petrovich Gnilidskii. . . . In the planning sessions with the director, those in charge of various sectors report not only on the fulfillment of their production tasks, but also on the moods . . . in their collectives. . . .[193]

A Party cadre will want to know the mood of the people, not in order to add it to other constraints on his actions, but in order to become aware of what it is precisely that he has to transform: "The manager must not . . . adapt himself to this or that mood [of his subordinates]."[194] The point is to make of an obstacle and a danger—some "spontaneous" mood—an *instrument*: a mood induced in those incapable of acting from "conscience."

Above "the masses" such ordinary human beings are—in what I surmise to be a predominating belief in higher Party levels—largely present in the "Party mass." Here again the point is to transform a negative into a positive factor: "The communists prepare themselves with anticipation (*volnenie*) for the receipt of new Party cards. The mood that now reigns among the members and candidates of the Party fosters the heightening of their activeness in production. . . . This mood is transmitted to the work collectives."[195]

* * * * * * * *

The mood to be created, from which the desired work performance flows, is an elation designated in a variety of ways.

The Party's aim may be "to create an *elevated mood* in people,"[196] or "to *give wings* to people."[197] Owing to the Party's impact, "the . . . collective lives a *full* (*polnokrovno*) life. . . . "[198] "It is necessary to create a mood such that everybody . . . experiences *joy of life*."[199] "We are striving for the wheat grower to travel to the field in a good mood as if it were on a *holiday*. . . . "[200]

The aim may be "to arouse enthusiasm in workers,"[201] "to make the Party's word . . . melt into working enthusiasm. . . . "[202] "Success [in

---

[193]G. Krivoshein, *PZh,* 1979, No. 16, p. 40.

[194]K. Chernenko 1978, p. 233.

[195]Unsigned article, *PZh,* 1972, No. 18, p. 37.

[196]A. Kurshakova, *PZh,* 1980, No. 4, p. 36.

[197]G. Krivoshein, *PZh,* 1978, No. 2, p. 18.

[198]V. Makarenko, *PZh,* 1979, No. 23, p. 47. Emphasis added.

[199]A manager, quoted in *PZh,* 1973, No. 16, p. 67. Emphasis added.

[200]B. Neletin, *P,* August 5, 1981. Emphasis added.

[201]Unsigned article, *PZh,* 1979, No. 14, p. 19.

[202]L. Brezhnev, at a Central Committee plenum, November 27, 1979, Brezhnev 1981a, p. 212.

agricultural production] depends on the ability of communists to fill the souls of people with enthusiasm."[203]

When the Virgin Lands had to be made fit for cultivation, "it was very important to *set all on fire*."[204] "Set people on fire to fulfill a task!"[205] "He was able to set people on fire and things got moving."[206] As high up as in a province Party organization, "the discussion of the books by Comrade L. I. Brezhnev provokes a . . . white heat (*nakal*) of work . . . [and] activeness."[207] It is also in "scientific institutes and development offices" that "Party collectives are charged with creating an atmosphere . . . of *nakal*."[208]

The central word for a sharp rise in performance flowing from an elation that "seizes one," "carries one away," is *pod'em*, surge: as at the front during the War "one rises [*podnyat'sya*] to the attack."[209] "Communists are obliged to constantly develop . . . an atmosphere of *pod'em* in production."[210] The aim is "to create in work collectives an atmosphere of . . . *pod'em*, of being carried away by the work. . . . "[211] The task of implementing the decisions of a Party congress, it is alleged, has led to "a *pod'em* that has seized our whole country."[212] Because of the imminence of another congress, "from the very first days of the new year . . . a *pod'em* reigns in the enterprise."[213] Recalling the reconstruction of a steel factory destroyed in the War (*Zaporzhstal*), Brezhnev arrives at the crucial moment: "An atmosphere emerged for which the Province Committee was striving from the beginning, an atmosphere of *pod'em* . . . I felt [thus]: a break has occurred and now we are going to go forward and forward."[214]

"The workers of the ideological front know how difficult it often is . . . to remove the existing inertia."[215] Only elation, the Party top suggests, is capable of surmounting the spontaneous reactions of ordinary people toward work. These are, at best, listlessness, sluggishness—hence "it is very important to know how to awake and

[203]V. Dolgikh, *PZh*, 1979, No. 13, p. 40.

[204]L. Brezhnev, *Tselina*, Brezhnev 1979, p. 167. Emphasis added.

[205]N. Virtsuk, *PZh*, 1978, No. 21, p. 78.

[206]V. Marisov, *P*, August 2, 1981.

[207]E. Kachalovskii, *PZh*, 1978, No. 11, p. 12.

[208]A. Kirilenko, *PZh*, 1978, No. 6, p. 15.

[209]L. Brezhnev, *Malaya zemla*, Brezhnev 1979, p. 16.

[210]Editorial, *PZh*, 1979, No. 14, p. 6.

[211]V. Oderov, *K*, 1973, No. 4, p. 74.

[212]K. Chernenko, *PZh*, 1976, No. 19, p. 8.

[213]K. Ulanov, *PZh*, 1981, No. 6, p. 63.

[214]L. Brezhnev, *Vozrozhdenie*, Brezhnev 1979, p. 83.

[215]D. Bibikov, *P*, November 2, 1981.

arouse people"[216] —and even (rarely mentioned) gloom. "When we entered the workshop, I almost physically felt . . . in the atmosphere . . . something uplifted, festive. *I did not see any gloomy faces.* Everyone had his holiday [about his own performance] every day, every month, every quarter. And all had a common holiday: the 9th Five-year Plan was fulfilled early! Everything was as in a festive demonstration."[217]

A bolshevik does not need to become elated to give his all to work. He feels a calm urge to do so in his unvaryingly sober mood, relishing the prospect of absorbing work: "Before us there is much work."[218] "As the saying goes, there surely is work to be done, something to which to apply one's forces."[219] "It is well known that work always was and will be the basis and the decisive factor of human life"[220]—a law, the violation of which causes disaster in the soul: "For a communist, life is unbearable without 'a load of work.'"[221]

Yet ordinary people, if left to themselves—the Party top appears to believe—are inclined to be indifferent toward work, or even to dislike it. Asked "what is for you the most difficult thing in the duties of management?", a manager answers, "to know how to draw people into work."[222] Proposing a favorable attitude toward work is the same as "opposing the love of work to spontaneity."[223] "I Work with Pleasure," a headline defiantly proclaims.[224]

The severity of the Soviet regime's reaction to those who flagrantly repudiate work may also express the Party top's horror and dismay over a more widespread and more prudent aversion toward work. "We all have to be *disturbed* by the fact that certain young, healthy people do not work and, *what is most important, do not wish to work.* These are the parasites. . . . The state applies the force of law to parasites."[225] For, as one may insist under the headline "We Shall

---

[216]Editorial, *PZh,* 1979, No. 14, p. 8.

[217]F. Robinov, *K,* 1975, No. 11, pp. 66–67. Emphasis added.

[218]Headline, *P,* January 4, 1982.

[219]N. Shagov, *P,* October 1, 1981.

[220]V. Shcherbitskii 1978, p. 113.

[221]A. Stakhanov, *P,* January 3, 1982.

[222]*P,* May 22, 1981.

[223]A. Titov and V. Kozyrenko, *PZh,* 1978, No. 15, p. 14.

[224]*Krasnaya Zvezda,* April 9, 1980.

[225]V. Shcherbitskii, speech, November 4, 1981, *Pravda Ukrainy,* November 5, FBIS, December 11, p. R-14. Emphasis added.

Work": "As Leonid Ilyich Brezhnev said, it is necessary to work. It is necessary to do things (*delat' delo*)."[226]

When a state of depression is replaced by a high, one's attraction to work supersedes one's aversion toward it: "There are those whose mood is buoyant, and then work goes swimmingly; there are others who feel lack of satisfaction, for whom work is no joy . . . "[227] and whose yield in work is low. When the country, in late 1980, is alleged to be looking forward elatedly to a Party Congress, "passion for work . . . characterizes the mood of the workers. . . . "[228] Beneath the pretense one detects a belief in what mood is required for intense work, when "inertia does not engulf people."[229] "If a decision [of the Party] does not 'touch one's innards,' does not arouse enthusiasm in the collective, it remains mere paper."[230] "Whoever does not burn, merely smolders."[231]

Just as performance in work should be maintained at a high level, incessantly and indefinitely (see Chap. VII), elation should be permanent. Thus an economic manager is beside the point when he observes (in a rare statement to appear in print) that "you can't move a serious affair by an outburst of enthusiasm."[232] For the elation aimed at or alleged to have been achieved by the Party leadership is a constant state of soul. When it is said about a model enterprise that "to such a collective, members go in the morning with elation,"[233] each and every morning is meant. While the Party top, of course, does not believe this to be often the case, it may well thus express a conviction about what is needed to induce high performance in work. "The everyday working life of the country is marked by a high . . . surge. . . . "[234] "Through the years of Soviet power, enthusiasm has transformed itself into a constantly operating factor."[235]

Left to themselves, workers are likely to shy away from work, feeling incapable of achievement. Brought into a state of elation, their then-emerging sense of high capacity tends, to be sure, to be spontaneously directed toward unrealistic objectives; but it can be channeled by the

---

[226]D. Obcharenko, *P*, April 4, 1982.

[227]Editorial note, *P*, January 21, 1980.

[228]Unsigned article, *PZh*, 1980, No. 22, p. 8.

[229]N. Pivovarov, *P*, December 31, 1981.

[230]V. Savchenko, *P*, October 18, 1981.

[231]N. Pivovarov, *P*, December 31, 1981.

[232]A. Ivanov, *P*, October 25, 1981.

[233]Editorial, *P*, January 16, 1982.

[234]Editorial, *P*, February 25, 1982.

[235]K. Chernenko 1980.

Party to aims that are both ambitious and attainable, by dint of intense work that has now turned from a burden to be avoided into a need to be satisfied. "Everything depends on mood—either a cat appears as a mountain or a mountain as a cat."[236] Now "we can handle anything." "When a person is in a good mood, he can move mountains."[237] It is up to the Party to direct such a sense of omnipotence to objectives that are—just barely—realizable (*napryazhenno nov polne real'no*) (see Chap. VI), so that the masses' mood will be "elevated, but also businesslike."[238]

In his normal state the ordinary person is dominated by "the wish for a *calm* life,"[239] which entails low performance; many are "those who search for the spot where there is most quiet and calm."[240] "What does it mean to look at one's conduct with severity? I believe it means always . . . to suppress in oneself the wish to sit quietly."[241] The Party top aims at replacing that wish with "a gust of passion in work":[242] "calm life has come to an end!"[243] "He is a person inclined toward doing. He does not look for a calm life."[244] His is an "unquiet calm (*bespokoinoe spokoistvie*)."[245]

The ordinary person in his ordinary state relishes a life that is easy and abhors one that is strenuous. "Man strives for an easier life,"[246] he "searches for easy places,"[247] he is "concerned with his own comfort."[248] "Whence comes the unwillingness of managers to take upon themselves high tasks requiring strenuous efforts? Perhaps from their striving to secure for themselves 'an easy life'?"[249] "The question always arises: how strenuous should the plan be? If one cares for one's calm, there is a simple path to it: to compose a plan with the smallest possible objective—the easiest to fulfill."[250] "Some managers, when encountering tasks whose fulfillment would be strenuous, strive to render their

[236]A. Chernyak, *P,* June 10, 1981.

[237]M. Voloshko, *PZh,* 1972, No. 18, p. 48.

[238]Editorial, *P,* April 7, 1980.

[239]Editorial, *PZh,* 1979, No. 14, p. 7. Emphasis added.

[240]A. Pelshe, speech, May 16, 1975, Pelshe 1978, p. 580.

[241]M. Poltoranin, *P,* May 16, 1981.

[242]I. Edneral, *P,* June 6, 1980.

[243]K. Khartsev, *PZh,* 1978, No. 16, p. 69.

[244]Editorial note, *P,* January 12, 1982.

[245]Headline, *P,* February 13, 1983.

[246]N. Umanets, *P,* March 14, 1980.

[247]B. Kornoplev, *P,* January 29, 1981.

[248]V. Lebedeva, *P,* January 14, 1982.

[249]G. Kolbin, *P,* June 5, 1981.

[250]I. Edneral, *P,* June 6, 1980.

life easier and begin proposing a reduction of the plan,"[251] a formula repeated by Brezhnev at the 26th Party Congress.[252] Or such managers underestimate the amount of work required for a certain yield. "Often one hears that in our region [the South] nature herself . . . guarantees large harvest. This is a superficial judgment. Bread is never and nowhere furnished easily!"[253] Rather, "in order to produce bread, much sweat must flow."

Ease is avoidance of *initiative.* "Apparently, for some officials of the Ministry our initiative entails a supplement of trouble: they would have to go to the Gosplan, to other organizations, strive to obtain resources, argue. Is it not simpler to wave the affair away?"[254]

Ease is avoidance of *conflict.* There is the cadre whose aim is "to create coziness where he himself bothers nobody and nobody bothers him."[255]

Ease is limiting one's efforts to steering clear of flagrantly violating explicit demands, to being middling rather than advanced. "Among the communists in our Party organizations . . . there are those who do not violate production or Party discipline, but [who] are hardly active members of the Party. . . . "[256] "Even among communists this opinion is still frequently present: I fulfill the obligations of my job, I do not violate discipline, I offend nobody—what then do you want of me?"[257] A communist accounts for his work to the Party meeting: "'My foreman has no criticisms of my work, I fulfill the norms, I do not violate discipline.' But, from the pronouncements of other communists, it resulted that Comrade Vergeichik does not overwork himself."[258]

In contrast, "He [the person conforming to the demands of the Party's top] Does Not Seek Easy Roads";[259] he adopts "plans that are not easy, that are strenuous."[260] "Of course, our plans are strenuous, but communists never put easy . . . tasks before themselves."[261] "The Soviet people, our Party," the Kremlin alleges, transforming an urge of the few into the deed of all, "lives a strenuous . . . life."[262]

---

[251]Editorial, *PZh,* 1979, No. 21, p. 4.

[252]L. Brezhnev 1981a, p. 691.

[253]L. Knetskov, *P,* December 7, 1982.

[254]I. Edneral, *P,* June 6, 1980.

[255]A. Pelshe, *K,* 1976, No. 15, p. 26.

[256]B. Vazhenin, *PZh,* 1978, No. 6, p. 36.

[257]V. Kozhenyako, *PZh,* 1979, No. 20, p. 26.

[258]N. Polozov, *PZh,* 1970, No. 7, p. 40.

[259]Headline, *P,* May 30, 1981.

[260]L. Brezhnev, quoted by K. Chernenko, *PZh,* 1976, No. 19, p. 8.

[261]V. Shcherbitskii, 1978, p. 281.

[262]Editorial, *PZh,* 1979, No. 14, p. 4.

There is no middle ground, the Party's top asserts, between strenuous work with a high yield and less strenuous work with negligible results: "*Any* amelioration of conditions of life can be obtained only by strenuous work. . . . "[263]

"To obtain any or all of this," one may observe about any good thing, "there has to be *kropotlivaya rabota,* painstaking work."[264] But another meaning of *kropotlivo* is "tedious." The Party's top is ever confronted with the divergence between its tastes and those of ordinary people.

"Strenuous" and "painstaking" work entails the surrendering of "all one's forces," "fully giving away one's forces without a remainder."[265]

In their common mood, ordinary people, the Party's top perceives, are intent upon conserving forces, loath to spend them, "aspiring to live by the principle of maximum economy of energy." But in elation, the expenditure of what is then felt no more as scarce, but rather as abundant, even inexhaustible, becomes a need. The point of inducing a high in people is "to make it possible for them to work with a full giving [*otdacha*] of their forces,"[266] "a giving of themselves,"[267] "without withholding anything."[268] Thus "the primary Party organizations of the factory Azovstal' . . . engendered the striving of all to work . . . with a maximal *otdacha* of forces."[269]

Alongside the ordinary person's resolve to limit effort goes his preference for routine, his aversion to change. He is apt to be dominated by "the sluggish force of inertia"[270] —the opposite of the pretended "all that's new to which . . . the masses give birth."[271] In fact, "important sectors of production and of services are headed by inert people."[272] When they abandon routine, it is not for long, "and then they forget about the innovation."[273] "Why, many economic managers ask, adopt new modes of production . . . if that is connected with diffi-

[263]L. Brezhnev, 26th Party Congress, March 3, 1981, Brezhnev 1981a, p. 734. Emphasis added.

[264]Editorial, *P,* September 30, 1980.

[265]*PZh,* 1978, No. 20, p. 18.

[266]G. Krivoshein, *PZh,* 1978, No. 2, p. 18.

[267]V. Bystrov, *P,* October 27, 1981.

[268]K. Chernenko 1980, p. 367.

[269]B. Kachura, *PZh,* 1979, No. 16, p. 15.

[270]Editorial, *PZh,* 1979, No. 14, p. 7.

[271]Editorial, *PZh,* 1977, No. 15, p. 11.

[272]V. Grishin, speech, September 14, 1977, Grishin 1979, p. 418.

[273]V. Sapega, *P,* December 12, 1982.

culties? Better to work in traditional fashion . . . [ellipsis in the text—NL]."[274] Such behavior may be hidden under a contrary mask: "There are people who proclaim the importance of working in a new manner who are in fact reconciled to inertness"[275]—or who even promote it by preserving incentives that obstruct change: "Enterprises are not always interested in rapidly adopting achievements of science and technology. To the directors of factories, it is often advantageous to utilize old techniques rather than adopting new ones. For to change technique it is necessary to reduce production for a time, to bear losses."[276]

How can the relationship of forces between "inertia," on the one hand, and "one of the most important manifestations of efficiency, the feeling for what is new," on the other, come to favor the latter? According to the Kremlin, by a change in people's mood. "The struggle for scientific-technical progress cannot be conducted with a cold heart: only by being carried away do the heights of economics become accessible. . . . "[277]

The ordinary person's heart may get hot when he feels his ordinary work "is connected with a great event."[278] That event may be one involving concrete and present personal benefit. "The occupancy of a new housing project [for workers] was imminent and, as always on the eve of a much expected event, there rolled a wave of elated animation through the workshop";[279] output rose.

Or, at the other extreme, the event may be a jubilee (*yubilei*); as when at the 24th Party Congress, Brezhnev looks back on the years since the 23d: "These were years of enormous . . . *pod'em* and enthusiasm for work on the part of Soviet people in connection with great anniversaries—the 50th Anniversary of the October Revolution and the 100th anniversary of the birth of V. I. Lenin. . . . "[280] A jubilee that should establish a connection between what in a normal mood would be the small work of little men and something great, whether man or happening—such a date becomes an "event" in its own right: "At present our Party and the whole country are on the eve of *events* of enormous significance such as the 150th birthday of Karl Marx [just a few months off—NL] and the 100th anniversary of the birth of

[274]V. Shcherbitskii, *PZh,* 1981, No. 15, p. 17.

[275]Editorial, *P,* January 28, 1980.

[276]A. Filatov, *P,* June 30, 1980.

[277]A. Brygin, *K,* 1982, No. 15, p. 70.

[278]L. Brezhnev, quoted in *PZh,* 1977, No. 6, p. 29.

[279]A. Ivanov, *P,* October 25, 1981.

[280]March 30, 1971, L. Brezhnev 1972, p. 195.

Vladimir Ilyich Lenin [more than two years away—NL]."[281] A jubilee is just as much of an event as a new occurrence: "The year 1982 will be full of big political events. There will be congresses of the trade unions and of the Komsomol. There will be elections to local Soviets. There will be the 60th anniversary of the Union of Socialist Soviet Republics. *All these events* will give an impulse for the further . . . *pod'em* in the . . . activeness of the masses."[282]

Such are the levers that a reliance on *pod'em* puts at the disposal of the Party's top—or so it pretends, if not half-believes.

DUTY (*DOLG*)

The dominant motive for work, so goes the Kremlin's well-known dictum, should be the conviction that a maximal personal contribution to production is everybody's duty, *dolg*, a word whose other meaning is "debt": "work as a . . . debt toward the Party . . ., the People . . ., Society. . . . "[283]

The Party leadership affirms that the Party should be and is making an ample effort to instill this preference. "Party organizations educate people to a conscious relationship toward their obligations, help the worker to be more deeply permeated by the common interest. . . . "[284] "We must persistently educate in people the feeling of intimate participation in the common cause, their interestedness in the general success."[285]

This endeavor is from time to time alleged to be already largely successful. "The basis of the people's heroism in work is above all . . . their feeling of a moral debt. . . . "[286] "Selflessness . . . in work . . . is characteristic for the overwhelming majority of Soviet persons."[287] "The number cited vividly characterizes the *razmakh* [scope, breadth] of our plans and deeds. Behind them is the selfless labor of millions of people. . . . "[288]

Sometimes the falseness of this contention is involuntarily implied: "The initiative of the Party group aimed at establishing creative

---

[281]L. Brezhnev, speech, February 16, 1968, Brezhnev 1970b, p. 177. Emphasis added.

[282]L. Brezhnev, speech at the plenum of the Central Committee, November 16, 1981, *P*, November 17. Emphasis added.

[283]K. Chernenko 1980, p. 366.

[284]G. Krivoshein, *PZh*, 1979, No. 16, pp. 38–39.

[285]A. Litovchenko, *P*, July 27, 1981.

[286]A. Kapto, *PZh*, 1976, No. 1, p. 27.

[287]G. Shilyaev, *PZh*, 1979, No. 1, p. 31.

[288]Editorial, *P*, July 27, 1981.

micro-brigades in the workshop; in them every worker will try to propose something valuable. This did not succeed with everybody. *But it was valuable enough* that the majority took fire with an unselfish striving. . . . "[289] "The Province Committee," one may say, combining the levers of *dolg* and of *pod'em*, "*strove to create* . . . an atmosphere which would lift the mood and the energy of the communists, work out their understanding of their *dolg*."[290] "We Soviet people *need* work, not from fear, but from conscience."[291]

Often actual conduct from *dolg* is presented in a way that implies its rarity. "Again and again I reflect on this initiative of Mukhdi Movsarovich. For nobody imposed this initiative on him—only his high sense of debt to the Party."[292] "Talk, for example, with the Zhdanov steelworker, Grigorii Yakovlevich Gorban, with . . . [further names of model workers—NL] . . . and you will feel a public-spirited concern for the common cause."[293] "The Party group organizer M. Zhdanov, together with the communist V. Ledin, remained behind after work to search for the defects. Nobody forced them, only their conscience as Party members."[294] "In the mail received by *Pravda*, . . . there are not a few letters in which . . . violations are asserted. The letter writer does not ask for anything for himself. He pleads for somebody else, defends general interests."[295] "What moves such people [model workers]? As a rule, they receive only little personal advantage from their activeness [in making proposals for improvements], their irreconcilability [toward defects]. Hence, both their thoughts and their acts are determined by something else—the striving to improve the common cause." "When distributing benefits, Ivanov is concerned in the first place with others and only secondarily with himself. He allots the best houses to workers; for them—not for himself!—he obtains sojourns in sanitoria. The director owns no cows, but one often sees him in the meadow with a goat. He helps the farmers to prepare their 'personal' hay. . . . To lead is for Ivanov always to think about people. Do we have many such Ivanovs. . . ? Fortunately, not a few." At the meeting of the bureau, a cadre addresses a worker: "I was touched to the depths of my heart by the sincere, even keen, care of yours not only, and even not so much, for your personal success

[289]A. Itigin, *P*, April 22, 1981.
[290]I. Senkin, *K*, 1971, No. 1, p. 24. Emphasis added.
[291]Yu. Malov, *P*, September 28, 1982.
[292]M. Bedernikov, *P*, January 10, 1982.
[293]V. Shcherbitskii, *P*, February 14, 1982.
[294]V. Bystrov, *P*, October 27, 1981.
[295]Editorial note, *P*, September 7, 1981.

as for the fate of the common cause. Accounting for your activity, you declared with all definiteness: personal success isn't worth much when matters around you do not go well."[296]

On the other hand, self-centered conduct may also be suggested to be rare; but I should expect the surprise that may be expressed upon encountering it (except in one who had been judged to be among the few selfless) to be rather feigned: "And then I convinced myself of this: This man is concerned only with his own indicators and not with the common ones."[297] Occasionally the prevalence of selfishness may be implied: "Now and then in the family and even in schools children are told about work as, above all, a means for satisfying material needs. More rarely is work spoken of as a duty, as an obligation, as an indispensable means for the development of society."[298]

* * * * * * * *

In several ways, the Party's top attempts to make work done out of *dolg* appear less remote from reality.

Maximizing one's contribution to production, it is stressed, also maximizes one's future income, even if income is not made dependent on performance. "To educate in people an attitude toward work for the good of society as one's . . . obligation" is also to educate them to recognize in work "the chief source of prosperity."[299] "The chief force of socialism . . . consists in this: all workers are interested in its successful development. . . . Socialism creates a direct material interest of the workers . . . in the most rapid development of production. . . . "[300] "Participating in socialist competition, every worker enjoys the possibility of showing by his deeds how deeply he has understood the dependence of his personal welfare . . . on his contribution to the common cause."[301]

Maximizing one's contribution to production is the same as maximizing one's own assets as a co-owner of all production: "The first concern of Party . . . organizations is to continuously educate in workers the feeling of being an owner (*khozyain*)."[302] "People can be divided

[296] *P*, January 16, 1983.

[297] V. Sapega, *P*, December 12, 1982.

[298] A. Silatov, *P*, November 11, 1982.

[299] A. Kosygin, at the 24th Party Congress, April 6, 1971, Kosygin 1979, Vol. 2, p. 44.

[300] Editorial, *K*, 1971, No. 18, p. 5.

[301] R. Musin, *PZh*, 1981, No. 21, p. 30.

[302] Editorial, *P*, July 17, 1980.

into two categories: the *khozyain* [owner] and the *postoronnii* [nonparticipant]. The *khozyain* keenly cares for the common cause. . . . "[303]

Maximizing the yield of one's work is also to "fully manifest one's capacities."[304] "Labor . . . reveals the . . . potential of individual development."[305] So far from depleting one, work is the best, no, the only proof of how capable one is. Work serves "the striving of man to disclose his capacity . . . ";[306] it is "where the worker can show his capacities."[307]

Maximizing work is tantamount to maximizing pleasure from the act of working. When the Party succeeds in educating men to "love of work," their "work turns into joy."[308] Man finds the "highest happiness in work."[309] Many will disagree—but "Party . . . organizations . . . have the mission to create . . . an atmosphere of deepest respect for the worker who loves work."[310]

"Already," one may say with unusual modesty, "for *many* Soviet persons work has become . . . the source of joyful life."[311] Yet it may seem prudent to be less exacting and instead to envisage creating "*the habit* of working as conscience commands,"[312] to achieve the condition where "the fulfillment of one's *dolg* to society transforms itself into a conscious habit."[313] Here the adjective still suggests the person's freedom of choice, but the forceful agent designated by the noun protects against the ill use of that capacity. "I make an effort to develop in myself . . . the habit of doing everything according to conscience. . . . "[314]

That is even more the case when there emerges a "*need* to live for others,"[315] or, when in a more prominent theme, work itself becomes a need: when working less than strenuously comes to devastate the ordinary person, as it probably would already affect many at the Party's top. "There was one salvation, one hope, one medicine: to work,"

---

[303]V. Lebedeva, *P*, January 14, 1982.

[304]V. Shcherbitskii, *PZh*, 1981, No. 15, p. 13.

[305]A. Kolesnichenko, *P*, May 19, 1981.

[306]Editorial, *K*, 1971, No. 14, p. 12.

[307]B. Neletin, *P*, August 5, 1981.

[308]R. Shalkin, *PZh*, 1978, No. 6, p. 31.

[309]K. Chernenko 1978, p. 249.

[310]Editorial, *P*, August 2, 1981.

[311]K. Chernenko 1978, p. 200. Emphasis added.

[312]G. Romanov, *K*, 1979, No. 8, p. 21. Emphasis added.

[313]V. Protopov, *K*, 1980, No. 6, p. 68.

[314]A young worker, quoted in editorial, *P*, March 15, 1983.

[315]G. Kononov, *P*, June 18, 1982.

Brezhnev reminisces about the conquest of the Virgin Lands.[316] "I cannot do otherwise."[317]

Perishing as the alternative to working strenuously is the prospect for all. "If, by some circumstance, people were deprived of the possibility of working, they would not only cease to advance in their physical and spiritual development, they would be condemned to degradation and degeneration."[318]

Yet, it seems to be implied, people may not be aware of the deterioration from too little work, or they may expect to suffer less from degenerating than the Party top. It is therefore up to the Party to make an effort, mostly unspecified, to ensure that a perfect performance in work becomes for everybody a "need" that is "deeply inner," "personal,"[319] "organic,"[320] "the most important existential necessity";[321] to ensure that "the soul" is "*obliged* to work."[322]

When this is accomplished, one's doubts about the "readiness of people to give all their forces for the common cause"[323] lose their pertinence: "When in the human being an urge toward work for society appears, then it becomes unnecessary to recall his *dolg* to him."[324] "The fulfillment of one's *dolg* will have become unavoidable (*neobkhodimost'*).[325] The omnipresence of initiative, for instance, will be assured by the prevalence of people "who literally *cannot live* without initiative."[326]

Then one can safely assert the corresponding *preference*: "In socialist society an attitude of initiative toward work becomes the first existential *need* of man, a moral *norm*."[327] Having shown that work is an existential need, one may also note its "incomparable beauty."[328]

Perhaps a high pitch of work must become a habit before it becomes a need. The Party should "ensure that . . . working to the full measure

---

[316]L. Brezhnev, *Tselina*, Brezhnev 1979, p. 178.

[317]Headline, *P*, July 7, 1982.

[318]K. Chernenko 1978, p. 200.

[319]L. Brezhnev, at a Central Committee plenum, December 16, 1974, Brezhnev 1976, p. 228.

[320]V. Shcherbitskii, *K*, 1980, No. 6, p. 31.

[321]Editorial, *K*, 1981, No. 1, p. 7.

[322]Title of an article by V. Kozhevnikov, *K*, 1979, No. 3, p. 46. Emphasis added.

[323]G. Krivoshein, *PZh*, 1979, No. 16, p. 38.

[324]I. Olkhovskii, *PZh*, 1980, No. 2, p. 69.

[325]V. Shcherbitskii, *K*, 1980, No. 6, p. 31.

[326]V. Koshenyako, *PZh*, 1979, No. 20, p. 25. Emphasis added.

[327]K. Chernenko 1978, p. 206. Emphasis added.

[328]Editorial, *P*, November 1, 1981.

of one's forces and capacities . . . be transformed into a habit, and then into the most important existential need."[329]

The first step to this end—the only one ever mentioned—is "the liquidation of manual, lowly skilled, and physically heavy work"; for "to solve this problem is to remove substantial obstacles from the path of the transformation of work into the first existential need of every person."[330]

But this ultimate objective is of so little immediate interest that it may also occasionally be alleged to have already been achieved: "The fulfillment of the decisions of the [25th Party] Congress *has become* the inner need of the workers in city and country."[331]

The evidence thus seems to confirm what the observer would expect: the Party's top does not rely on *dolg* as a major motive for work by the masses.

* * * * * * * *

In this connection, the Kremlin is faced, decade in and decade out, by the massive violation of a more modest norm: that of accepting responsibility for specific operations inherent in one's job, ordered by superiors, accepted in agreements, or announced in one's initiatives. As is well known, both negligence and violations of proper conduct for an ulterior purpose appear to the Kremlin increasingly to be major obstacles to the fulfilment of its designs.

"The feeling of responsibility for an honest fulfillment of the duties of his office got blunted in him":[332] an all too expected event, as an initial deficiency in such feelings would also have been. The noun *neobyazatel'nost'* denotes low attachment to conforming one's conduct to one's obligations. The Party top frequently observes the occurrence of *bezotvetsvennost'* [lack of responsibility], *nedistsiplinirovannost'* [lack of discipline], *neorganizovannost'* [lack of organization], and "the absence of elementary order."[333] "I could never understand those whom it costs nothing to violate their word. You agree with such a one about a meeting, you wait a whole hour, and the next day he explains, without any embarrassment: I couldn't find the time, I was

---

[329]L. Brezhnev, at the 25th Party Congress, quoted in *K*, 1979, No. 6, p. 37.

[330]L. Brezhnev, speech at the 26th Party Congress, February 21, 1981. Brezhnev 1981a, p. 700.

[331]L. Brezhnev, at a Central Committee plenum, October 25, 1976. Brezhnev 1978, p. 138.

[332]K. Minakov, *PZh*, 1982, No. 2, p. 56.

[333]M. Suslov, *PZh*, 1979, No. 21, p. 18.

busy. . . . [ellipsis in the text—NL]."[334] "'It will be done!' some readily answered and then did nothing."[335]

Here, it may be observed, against the background of the regime's aspirations to create virtuous habits, is a vicious one that *is* taking: "Disorder in everything—at home, at work—has this strange property: one gets accustomed to it.[336]

In early Andropov the classical Russian comparison between one's own disorder and German order reappears: "Take, for instance, the pressing workshop No. 1 of the Moscow automobile factory in the name of the Leninist Komsomol in which I work. For a long time everything here seemed good to me, in order. Surely I would never have written a letter to *Pravda*, had there not been a certain event in my life. Recently I sojourned at length abroad; I participated in the familiarization with new equipment which had been prepared in the GDR at the order of our enterprise. One thing is certain: there is more order there than in our pressing workshop. I told my new German worker friends [about our advanced workers] . . . I told everything. If something happens, [our workers] come to the factory on a Saturday or on a Sunday, remain without rest for two shifts. This happened more than once. They rescued the factory. At this point, the German friends interrupted me and asked the translator to translate more precisely. What does this mean 'something happens?' And what is it to 'rescue the factory?' Can there be any accidents in a well-arranged enterprise? And what extraordinary causes could force a chief of a workshop to come to the factory on a holiday and even to call workers? Is that order?"[337]

In early Andropov it also becomes possible to admit that a violation may be committed not for the transgressor's good but for that of his "collective." "Some managers attempt to justify . . . fictitious accounts [*pripiski*] . . . financial machinations . . . by the interest of their mission."[338] What is more, their sincerity is accepted when it is added that "we severely condemn such a lack of principle."[339] Similarly, a chairman of a kolkhoz "did not learn to respect the law. . . . In order, for instance, to obtain some advantage for the kolkhoz, he did not refrain from having recourse to corruption. He believed that to obtain a com-

---

[334]V. Sotnichenko, *P*, March 20, 1982.

[335]L. Brezhnev, *Tselina*, Brezhnev 1979, p. 163.

[336]L. Kalachkov, *P*, April 18, 1983.

[337]Ibid.

[338]S. Mukashev, *P*, December 16, 1982.

[339]Ibid.

mon aim [it was not for himself that he was striving!—NL] all means are good."[340]

Violations may be condemned in ways that suggest their prevalence as well as their moral acceptability. "Socialist competition, the members of the plenum declared, is incompatible with . . . fictitious accounts. . . . "[341] "A business-like person will never consent to *pripiski*. . . .[342]

In early Andropov it is disclosed that there is an entire sector, that of distribution, where people with a "large spoon" dominate: "They establish their rules, dictate their conditions."[343]

Punctiliousness in the discharge of one's obligations, a keen feeling for them, is a rare excellence. "*Obyazatel'nyi chelovek* [a person who takes his obligations seriously]" is the headline of an editorial according to which "of him people say, you can set your watch by him."[344] "When you give him a mission, you know beforehand that it is going to be fulfilled in good time and with a striving for perfection."[345] "What distinguishes the propagandists of the factory? Above all, a responsible attitude toward their mission."[346] "Many enterprises and branches of production have assembled not a little experience in the fulfillment of orders in full conformity with economic agreements. . . . " "Not accidentally, this enterprise [a model one] . . . for the Five-Year Plan period does not admit disruption in deliveries."[347] The headline "A Contract Is Dearer Than Money" may be thus illustrated:" "When it comes to composing a list of the best factories [in the country], undoubtedly one of the first places will be occupied by the factory ATE-1. Why? There are enterprises that are larger and more famous. But for all the years of the 10th Five-Year Plan, this factory has not paid a single ruble in penalties for the violation of economic contracts."[348]

Only rarely is it observed that thus the elementary has become meritorious. "Sometimes one even has to hear that somebody 'came forward with the initiative to obey technological discipline strictly.' That is, the fulfillment of elementary production obligations is raised to the

[340]M. Poltoranin, *P*, March 15, 1983.

[341]Unsigned article, *PZh*, 1982, No. 11, p. 26.

[342]A. Nikitin, *P*, May 17, 1982.

[343]N. Feokitostov, *P*, January 20, 1983.

[344]*P*, April 4, 1982.

[345]V. Dashyan, *P*, May 6, 1981.

[346]V. Zhitenev, *P*, September 20, 1981.

[347]Editorial, *P*, April 25, 1983.

[348]V. Parfenov, *P*, May 4, 1981.

rank of eminent merit."[349] "At times the simplest rules, universally known obligations without which production is unthinkable, are presented as something new."[350] "In some individual plans [of workers] there are many points, but only one or two concrete ones. The rest is general words, matter-of-course requirements of the type 'to fulfill production tasks . . . [ellipsis in the original—NL].'"[351]

In these conditions it continues to seem appropriate to point out that orderliness does have its *advantages*: "The path to high quality of work is . . . organizedness and order in production."[352] "Life convinces [one]: where there is more order in production . . . there, results are better."[353] "It is not hard to imagine how much the results of every [work] collective's activity would improve if each and every member did everything he was supposed to do. . . . The successful functioning of our national economic organism can only be ensured if everyone carries out the duties of his job or post."[354]

The Party top insistently *demands* that people discharge their obligations. "But what is indispensable above all is elementary order,"[355] "precise order in . . . work processes, the disciplined conduct in the first place of communists . . .,"[356] "a responsible attitude . . . toward contractual obligations."[357] One recalls that "every worker, and above all every leader, is obliged to fulfill the task that has been entrusted to him."[358]

It is thus a *central* objective "to make an honest attitude toward work the norm of the life of every Soviet person,"[359] to foster "qualities necessary for Party, Soviet, and economic work such as strict fulfillment of tasks."[360]

The Party is still *expending much effort* to this end. An objective in organizing operations is "that every . . . link, every worker . . . precisely fulfill the function that has been entrusted to him."[361] In the famous metallurgical *kombinat* at Magnitogorsk "a few years ago, the steel

---

[349]N. Kirichenko, *P*, May 26, 1980.

[350]A. Brygin, *K*, 1982, No. 15, p. 63.

[351]A worker, quoted in *P*, January 16, 1983.

[352]Editorial, *P*, February 11, 1982.

[353]Editorial, *P*, March 30, 1982.

[354]I. Pomelev, *P*, May 29, 1981.

[355]Editorial, *K*, 1979, No. 8, p. 5.

[356]G. Smaglienko, *PZh*, 1979, No. 5, p. 40.

[357]Editorial, *P*, November 1, 1981.

[358]G. Smaglienko, *PZh*, 1982, No. 9, p. 52.

[359]Editorial, *P*, August 2, 1981.

[360]K. Chernenko 1980, pp. 365–366.

[361]V. Shcherbitskii 1978, p. 33.

worker, M. Ilin, called on his comrades at a Party meeting to furnish all steel strictly according to orders. The significance of this step was big. . . . The movement begun by M. Ilin continues (and develops!) with great economic effect until this day."[362] Indeed, "the most basic aspect of work with personnel is educating them to an honest attitude toward their missions."[363] "For economic managers to feel keenly responsible for their missions, the staffs of the city or district committees must teach them this quality. . . . "[364]

This is the case even for types of personnel whom Westerners would expect to be little moved to disregard duties. "Special attention was directed to the heightening of the responsibility of leading cadres for conformity with plan discipline."[365] As to "the governmental *kontrol'*-inspection apparatus in which a considerable number of communists are occupied," "Party organizations are obliged to *educate* in these communists an irreconcilable attitude toward any attempts to deceive the government."[366]

If only the urge to violate could be replaced by the need to conform: "The necessity of impeccable, honest work must acquire irreversible force, become a need."[367] Generally, "for every Soviet person, conformity with the norms of social morality and law must be a natural need. . . . "[368]

Thus it appears as difficult to obtain conformity to the minimum requirement of discharging manifest obligations as it is to make people heed the maximum requirement of selflessness.

All the more so, as violators are encouraged by what amounts to widespread complicity rather than dissuaded by the appeal to "irreconcilability." "Negligence in the fulfillment of one's manifest obligations . . . becomes more frequent . . . [and] meets ever and ever . . . softer reactions."[369] "In some enterprises, violators of discipline feel themselves in freedom. . . . "[370] There are many current expressions of a "penchant to forgive all": "Well, so a human being erred," "but life is life, all kinds of things happen in it."

Against such a spontaneous disposition, the leadership requires that every conduct be given "an evaluation from principle"—in preference

---

[362] A. Litovchenko, *P*, July 27, 1981.

[363] A. Sushkov, *P*, November 11, 1981.

[364] E. Muravyev, *P*, August 12, 1982.

[365] F. Meshkov, *PZh*, 1981, No. 11, p. 29.

[366] K. Chernenko 1980, p. 252.

[367] Editorial, *P*, November 1, 1981. Emphasis added.

[368] Editorial, *P*, September 29, 1982.

[369] Editorial, *K*, 1982, No. 16, p. 9.

[370] Editorial, *P*, February 2, 1983.

to evoking a response based on empathy or sympathy, if not on an interest in not "spoiling relations." It is one of the Party's tasks "to educate to intolerance toward any violation of any rule."[371]

A difficult endeavor. For to the question "Is it easy to be irreconcilable?"[372] the answer is: "Nobody says that it is easy to be irreconcilable. No!"[373] For, as a worker reports, "the managers . . . picked me to pieces, tried to present me as a 'scribbler,' a 'complainer,' only because I came out with an article"[374]—a reaction probably shared by many of the worker's peers and transformed into its opposite by the official voice according to which "his passionate irreconcilability toward defects brought him the deep respect of his colleagues. . . . "[375]

MATERIAL STIMULATION

If the Party leadership exalts work done in the spirit of *dolg*, this does not prevent it from stressing material interests.

As we would expect, one of these positions remains unmentioned when the other is expressed. It is rare to make "educational work by the Party"—for *dolg*—into "the second path of struggle" while "the first element of action" is "to adopt . . . an economic mechanism that . . . not only does not favor bureaucratism, but deters it."[376]

But one may include both accents within the same pronouncement on condition of making them distant from each other. Early in an article one may observe that "only a person who gives his entire self to the common cause lives in dignity,"[377] and later "economic stimuli . . . are indispensable. To build communism on the enthusiasm of toilers only is a utopia."[378] What is disclosed here is the esoteric Bolshevik belief that until the coming of communism the masses are bound to lack dignity.

It is mostly authors who present themselves as economists or economic managers who, at least in the view of their opponents, "show

[371]L. Gorshkov, *P*, February 19, 1983.

[372]Headline, *Pravda*, January 5, 1983.

[373]N. I. Matafonov, *P*, January 5, 1983.

[374]Ibid.

[375]Editorial note, ibid.

[376]M. Mikhailov, *K*, 1981, No. 8, pp. 107–108.

[377]K. Chernenko, *K*, 1982, No. 6, p. 31.

[378]Loc. cit., p. 40.

condescension toward measures of moral stimulation and rely chiefly on material stimuli."[379]

Yet Party voices may also affirm that "guaranteeing supplementary profit [to an enterprise] for better work is the real lever for heightening effectiveness."[380] "One must . . . utilize the economic mechanism . . . so as to render all working people . . . from rank-and-file workers to commanders of production interested in the maximal utilization of reserves of production."[381] "The system . . . of material stimulation should be constructed so that the workers of every link [become] interested in bringing to the user as large an amount of production as possible, and of production of high quality."[382] "Any large-scale program can be implemented only if the people implementing it . . . have a personal interest in the achievement of high results."[383] "Every worker should see and feel the . . . connection between what he has done and what he has earned."[384]

Those who speak for the supreme authority, or who are of it, may admit that producers' incomes are insufficiently dependent on their performance, which suffers in consequence: "It occurs that salaries essentially depend on the mere presence at the place of work, and not on its real results . . . this has extremely harmful effects on . . . production. . . . "[385] "Today the worker knows that, whether he has fulfilled his task or not, his wage will be approximately the same."[386]

Where an economic result is negative, the cause may be found in the pricing of factors having been made too little dependent on performance. "Some time ago . . . [certain] workshops in the factory did not fulfill their production objectives. . . . Here defects in the system of material stimulation were tolerated. This inhibited . . . the striving of people to . . . fulfill their . . . tasks."[387] "What is the cause of the low level of fulfillment of production orders? It is that the . . . indicators for the evaluation of the activity of enterprises and the systems for

---

[379]B. Neletin, *P*, August 5, 1981.

[380]Yu. Yakobets, *K*, 1979, No. 6, p. 81.

[381]Editorial, *K*, 1974, No. 11, p. 4.

[382]L. Brezhnev, at the Central Committee plenum, July 1979, quoted in I. Syroezhin, *K*, 1980, No. 14, p. 40.

[383]M. Gorbachev, *K*, 1982, No. 10.

[384]L. Brezhnev, speech, May 24, 1982, FBIS, May 25, p. R-10—words substantially repeated by Yu. Andropov.

[385]L. Brezhnev, speech at the 26th Party Congress, February 23, 1981. Brezhnev 1981a, p. 702.

[386]Yu. Kuznetsov, quoted by V. Kuzmishchev, *P*, March 23, 1983.

[387]V. Smirnov, *PZh*, 1973, No. 4, p. 44.

determining premiums still only weakly orient work collectives toward the timely and entire fulfillment of orders."[388] "What hinders [a rise in the quality of shoes] is . . . the absence of material responsibility of managers for unsatisfactory work of their enterprises"[389]—a finding of the Party identical with that made by an economic manager: "I often wonder why several levels of authority issue dubious orders with such ease. I explain it by the fact that the material stimuli for planners . . . are badly connected with final economic results."[390]

One may note perverse incentives. "As the experience of recent years shows, enterprises issuing dated products often continue as before to find themselves in a more advantageous economic position than collectives that . . . adopt new techniques. The . . .encouragement [premium] for an increase in the quality of products often does not compensate for the costs incurred, and the receipt of such encouragement . . . is obtained [only] with much difficulty, after lengthy correspondence with the pertinent ministry, Gosplan, and the Ministry of Finance of the USSR."[391] "To introduce a . . . new technology, production has to be reorganized. . . . You may be taken to task for failing production plans, but only scolded, at the most, for not introducing new technology."[392] "Among the foremen of our enterprises there are some whose professional knowledge is insufficient. Here is one effect of the inappropriateness in the salaries of foremen, who often earn less than highly qualified workers. . . . "[393] "It happens that penalties are imposed on a manager . . . who assumes a risk and sometimes fails. But premiums are obtained by those who work tepidly, are excessively cautious, and overinsure themselves."[394]

It may be shown that performance improves as the dependence of income on performance rises. "It is as if people had changed," remarks a chief of factory section upon the introduction of the "brigade" system of payment. "Now everybody treasures the working hour [and] there are no absentees anymore."[395] "Some workers began to leave their shift prematurely. That troubled the communists. On the proposal of the Party group, the Administration transferred the majority of the workers to piece-work pay. From then on . . . the number of violations of

[388]Editorial, *P*, February 12, 1983.

[389]Editorial, *P*, February 11, 1982.

[390]L. Burtsev, *P*, October 5, 1981.

[391]Editorial, *K*, 1973, No. 3, p. 6.

[392]Yu. Andropov, Central Committee plenum, November 22, 1982, FBIS, November 23, p. R-4.

[393]I. Polyakov, *PZh*, 1973, No. 4, p. 12.

[394]V. Shcherbitskii, *PZh*, 1981, No. 15, p. 14.

[395]V. Kormushin and others, *P*, April 24, 1980.

work discipline diminished sharply"—which shows how an income stimulus works? No, rather, how "the Party group becomes an acting force."[396]

There are recurring demands for sharpening the dependence of income on performance. "The violators of plans of enterprises and of agreements between them should be punished sharply by the ruble."[397] "In the construction industry, economic levers should be worked out and adopted which would induce managers . . . to spend their resources economically."[398] "The interest of collectives in the growth of the quality of products should be heightened. Today . . . expenditures on heightening the durability and reliability of products are [seldom compensated for] by [increases in the] prices of goods of a higher category."[399] "It is necessary . . . to make the payment of particular workers depend ever more directly on the final results of their activity."[400] There should even be a "strengthened dependence of the pay of every scientist on his . . . contributions to . . . scientific-technical progress."[401] Observing that productivity suffers if one cannot lose one's job because of low performance, an author may judge it "above all, important that everybody, whether worker, engineer, or manager of any rank, cherish his working place . . . and hence, work with maximum yield."[402] In sum, and according to one from whom one might not have expected these words: "One cannot . . . agree with the opinion of some research workers, and even of [some] managers, that the role of wages as a stimulation for work is declining. Life requires the heightening of the stimulating role of wages."[403]

* * * * * * * *

Thus year after year the Party's top judges the degree to which the income stimulus is applied to be insufficient, but so it remains. A major cause of this discrepancy is familiar to Western analysts: the more effective the "economic mechanism," the more difficult it becomes to allege and justify the Party's "leading role" in the economy.

This conflict of interest causes the Party leadership to attach numerous reservations to its advocacy of "material stimulation." These I shall now survey.

---

[396]A. Murashov, *PZh*, 1979, No. 4, pp. 57–58.

[397]Editorial, *P*, January 3, 1980.

[398]Editorial, *K*, 1973, No. 3, p. 10.

[399]Editorial, *P*, August 19, 1981.

[400]A. Murashov, *PZh*, 1979, No. 4, pp. 57–58.

[401]Editorial, *K*, 1971, No. 18, p. 9.

[402]A. Chekalin, *P*, January 26, 1983.

[403]M. Suslov, *K*, 1981, No. 11, p. 7.

* * * * * * * *

It is exceedingly rare to admit the conflict between working from *dolg* and for income: "By the style of our life we are educating . . . the man of the coming communist society; but with remuneration of work depending on performance we are creating individualist strivings in him."[404]

Rather, one may, without elaborating, assert on occasion the reality of "dedication *combined with* material interestedness."[405] "All the good things a Soviet person does, he accomplishes *both* for himself and for . . . society";[406] "he works for himself *and* for his society."[407]

If roles are assigned to the components of that combination, the ordinary may turn out to be a mere instrument for the noble. "When a brigade has its own accounting (*khozraschet*) . . . there emerges a collective interestedness in the final results of work. A result of this is a favorable moral-psychological climate."[408] "Encouragement [income benefits] must heighten the striving to work even better for the common good."[409]

A word may straddle the two motives, suggesting the high while allowing for the low: "The socialist principle of distribution depending on the quantity and quality of work . . . incites the masses to work with an even greater *giving* of their forces."[410]

Having shown the benefits to be derived from an enhancement of the income stimulus, one may conclude a statement with the suggestion that *pod'em* and *dolg* had also operated:

> During the last years . . . measures have been adopted aimed directly at reducing the mobility of personnel. With this aim, for instance, rewards have been introduced for having served for certain time periods, depending on the length of uninterrupted work. In many enterprises supplementary vacations have been introduced . . . depending on the length of uninterrupted work. The realization of measures indicated in the decisions of the 24th and 25th Party Congresses [and] the plenums of the Central Committee, statements of Comrade L. I. Brezhnev, [and] *the strengthening of political-educational work* have permitted . . . reduction in the mobility of personnel.[411]

---

[404]B. Odlis, *K*, 1980, No. 1, p. 79.

[405]G. Kreslavskii, *PZh*, 1975, No. 2, p. 34. Emphasis added.

[406]G. Krivoshein, *PZh*, 1979, No. 16, p. 39. Emphasis added.

[407]L. Brezhnev, 26th Party Congress, March 3, 1981. Brezhnev 1981a, p. 735. Emphasis added.

[408]R. Musin, *PZh*, 1981, No. 21, p. 28.

[409]V. Vorovkov, *PZh*, 1979, No. 12, p. 32.

[410]M. Suslov, *PZh*, 1981, No. 8, p. 21. Emphasis added.

Correspondingly, the costs incurred from too little income stimulus may be perceived (or presented) as if the operation of *pod'em* or *dolg* had been impaired. "When practically everybody obtains *premiums* in the same measure, although one really does the work and the other . . . runs away from it . . . such a practice spoils enthusiasm."[412] "It happens that the contribution of engineers to the common cause is neglected; its moral and material encouragement is not provided for. This reduces the enthusiasm of specialists for work."[413]

Having income depend on performance may be presented as a matter of morality rather than efficiency.

"Earlier it was thus," one may observe in a rare mention of change, "workers received premiums inconspicuously with their wages. Today premiums are awarded solemnly, those receiving them are thanked for their honest work. . . . [In the words of a receiver], 'a premium is not merely money earned, but a sign of respect for one's work.'"[414] "Where premiums are distributed according to merit," as they always should be, "they are received as a public recognition of a contribution to the development of production."[415] "What is"—that is, ought to be—"important is not so much the reward as the attention shown to the person."[416]

To make income depend on performance may be presented as an act of distributive justice rather than as a measure of economic efficiency. Economists are permitted to point out that "receiving a part of society's riches depending on the quality and quantity of the work which has been given to society is not only the most just principle of distribution, but also the most effective one";[417] that where the principle of the dependence of wage on input is violated, "not only is substantial damage inflicted on justice, but work discipline falls, the productivity of work is diminished, economic growth is inhibited."[418] But to the Party leadership "paying every member of socialist society in accordance with the productivity of his labor is," in the first place, "indissolubly connected with . . . justice. . . . "[419] If "it is impossible . . . to agree with the opinion of some scientists and even of some economic managers that, as a lawful development in socialism, the role

[411] N. Tikhonov, *K*, No. 3, 1980, p. 6. Emphasis added.

[412] G. Romanov, *K*, 1981, No. 16, p. 18. Emphasis added.

[413] Editorial, *P*, December 18, 1981.

[414] Editorial, *P*, June 1, 1981.

[415] Editorial, *P*, June 1, 1981.

[416] V. Vorovkov, *PZh*, 1979, No. 12, p. 35.

[417] N. Rimashevskaya and E. Yasin, *P*, June 2, 1981.

[418] Ibid.

[419] A. Pelshe, *K*, 1981, No. 11, p. 6.

of wages in the stimulation of work is weakening," if rather "in reality, life requires an increase in the stimulating role of wages," it is "so as to exclude . . . violations of the *just* principle of closing the chinks against nonwork income, against idlers and all lovers of an easy livelihood."[420] "One must . . . encourage honest workers, leave no loopholes for loafers and purveyors of faulty work to live the good life while furnishing worthless work. Whoever wants to live well must work more and better."[421] "Our system of material . . . stimuli must establish . . . a just evaluation of everybody's contribution."[422] "An honest worker cannot but be *indignant* when he is . . . treated like somebody who does nothing"[423]—and might then even perform less well.

Thus income might depend on performance, while that performance itself springs from *dolg*: "The . . . principle of socialist society 'from each according to his capacity, to each according to his work' means that every working person . . . works for the common good . . . and receives his work according to its quantity and quality."[424]

When "material stimulation" and its intended effect on production are discussed, the motive through which such encouragement would achieve its desired sequel—the striving to enhance income—is likely to be left unmentioned by Party voices (in contrast to those who speak as economists).

It is rare for Party voices to find no apparent evil in "honestly striving for a rise [in income],"[425] in "the natural striving to earn as much as possible."[426] It is exceptional for members of a sovkhoz to be quoted as remarking, "The new head understands the working man. . . . He permits him to earn (*dat'zarabotat'*). . . . "[427]

When the aspiration to earn more *is* mentioned, it is likely to be disapproved of by Party voices. "Seekers for personal advantage, persons enterprising (*predpriimchevyi*) [an adjective which is also in favorable use—NL], and greedy. . . . "[428] "The mediocre person is self-

---

[420]M. Suslov, *K*, 1981, No. 16, pp. 7–8. Emphasis added.

[421]Words of L. Brezhnev at the 26th Party Congress, paraphrased in the editorial, *PZh*, 1981, No. 6, p. 10.

[422]L. Brezhnev, at the 26th Party Congress, February 23, 1981. Brezhnev 1981a, p. 702.

[423]K. Chernenko, *K*, 1982, No. 6, p. 42. Emphasis added.

[424]Resolution of the Central Committee for the 110th birthday of Lenin, quoted in Suslov, *K*, 1980, No. 4, p. 17.

[425]A model worker, quoted by V. Parfenov, *P*, January 2, 1980.

[426]R. Luts, *P*, August 15, 1981.

[427]N. Zenkovich, *P*, June 27, 1981.

[428]Yu. Kolesnikov, *P*, February 4, 1982.

seeking in a grabbing way."[429] "The severe reaction of Party organizations in all cases where a person . . . is guided only by motives of personal advantage . . . is fully justified."[430] "If you work assiduously, but make an effort only for your own pocket . . . do not expect to be respected by your comrades."[431] "This man, Marchenko [a model Party member] understood, had only accidentally [inappropriately—NL] come to the big construction; he is looking only for his own advantage."[432] After all, "one encounters even worker-tutors who work only 'for the ruble.'"[433] "When determining the outcome of socialist competition, we should . . . study more deeply the motives for work. . . . Had the common interest of the Party, the government, the people become the very own interest of the winner? Or did he above all pursue his personal interest?"[434] "Sometimes what wins out in a person is not the motive of conscious creativity, but rather the desire to earn more . . . taking no account of the norms of our life."[435] He may indeed forget about these "norms," considering only what the law allows:

> The communists of the workshop at a meeting criticized a comrade . . . for the fact that he was in all things governed by material interest. But he, a capable . . . specialist, took offense, mounted on the speaker's platform and said, "Do I fulfill the shift norm? I do fulfill it. Do I receive premiums? I do receive them. Thus it is shown that I conform to Party regulations. As to the rest about which you are talking, that is a matter of character. One person has his pockets full of enthusiasm, but I prefer rubles there. Party regulations do not hinder any one of us." The entire meeting had to prove to him that he had misunderstood the Party statute. He had seen the letter, but [had] not penetrated to the spirit. . . . [ellipses in the original—NL].[436]

If the hankering after income is to be nonevil, it may have to be kept secondary: "There is nothing reprehensible in the striving of a person to have, let us say, a good apartment, to earn more, to care for his family. But it is important to ask: has this not become your main aim in life. . . ?"[437]

---

[429]L. Brezhnev, quoted by N. Tikhonov, *K*, 1980, No. 3, p. 4.

[430]V. Grishin, *PZh*, 1972, No. 1, p. 15.

[431]V. Vinogradov, *P*, March 24, 1980.

[432]V. Smirnov, *P*, January 7, 1982.

[433]Yu. Malov, *P*, September 28, 1982.

[434]N. Zenkovich, *P*, June 27, 1981.

[435]G. Kononov, *P*, June 18, 1982.

[436]V. Safonov, *P*, March 20, 1983.

[437]Editorial, *P*, February 11, 1982.

High performance does not excuse striving for income. "Often this happens: a worker has obtained high indicators. . . . But . . . sometimes it turns out that he is only a sham advanced worker, because he works only for the ruble, but not at all for the interests of the collective."[438] "I am meeting . . . 'heroes' of a certain kind even among members of the Party. Such a person knows his business, and works, as the saying goes, without unbending. But what is often his aim? Money, a car, a house at which all will gape. . . ? Only for himself. . . . "[439] [ellipses in the original—NL].

High performance may even be felt to aggravate the sin of striving for income—and so a valuable potential combination of good motive and high capacity may go unrealized. "We cannot be satisfied even with the highest results of work if at its base there lies . . . the striving for personal enrichment. . . . "[440] "A high professionalism of a person is only one side of the matter. Not less important is . . . from what motives he acts, social ones or . . . personal . . . ones. . . . "[441] "Sisenko," the secretary of a factory's Party committee says in describing a worker, "has golden hands, but sometimes I am simply ashamed for him: in all things he has a personal calculation. You know why he goes to other workshops? In order to increase his pay."[442]

Those who are *strongly* striving for income, it is alleged, are likely to be striving *only* for it, and "look at work only as a necessity so as to receive money."[443] "Sometimes a person arrives at the factory, and very soon it becomes clear: nothing except money interests him here."[444] "Recently the sovkhoz received a new truck. Whom should one place in it? Clearly, Pavel Antonovich. Rudinskii went around the track. . . . 'An excellent machine,' he said. 'Only I shall continue in my own.' But, the people around him said, 'the pay with the new one is bigger, you are a strange fellow. . . . '" The people who are speaking thus are "those who look on work only as something that cannot be avoided so as to receive money. . . . " Such people "call eccentrics those whose reaction to work is different."[445]

Those who strive for more pay are also likely to be those who attempt to furnish less work, "people who are . . . concerned with one thing only: how to give as little as possible and grab as much as

[438] E. I. Kalaichev, *P*, October 20, 1982.

[439] A worker, quoted in *P*, January 16, 1983.

[440] Editorial, *K*, 1972, No. 11, p. 13.

[441] P. Masherov, *K*, 1978, No. 16, p. 12.

[442] A. Zolin, *P*, April 27, 1980.

[443] N. Zenkovich, *P*, June 27, 1981.

[444] V. Vakhnin, *P*, June 1, 1980.

[445] N. Zenkovich, *P*, June 27, 1981.

possible. . . . "[446] "People [exist] who do not think above all about the job to be done, but rather about finding . . . a loophole so as to live well while furnishing only a small effort."[447] "There are mothers who dress up a school girl like a bride. Her ring is of gold, her shoes the most modish ones and her dress expensive. . . . I don't believe that such a swell will become a good worker."[448]

Those striving for income are as little likely to heed the law as to heed morality. Confronted with reports of persons who have refrained from maximizing their income, "there have been people who have greeted this [information] with lack of understanding or even with laughter. Who are they? I imagine they are the same [ones] who know how to procure advantages for themselves everywhere. Never mind by what means."[449] "A person is rising on the ladder of positions, nobody sees anything bad in him—he is energetic, not without abilities. But then he becomes a mediocrity who thinks more about acquiring a 'Zhiguli' or fashionable clothes. . . . [ellipsis in the original—NL.] *And from there it is only one step to fraud.*"[450]

"In our brigade a majority of workers have been working for ten or more years. [One of the reasons is that,] *I'm not going to hide it,* salaries are decent—higher than at the neighbors."[451] In the atmosphere described, it is indecent to talk in public about what one earns—a difficulty encountered by Andropov when he apparently tried to break this taboo:

> The General Secretary of the Central Committee of the CPSU, Yu. Andropov, visited the Moscow machinebuilding factory in the name of Sergo Ordzhonikidze. Yu. V. Andropov interested himself in the situation of the personnel. The director of the factory, M. S. Chikirev, answered that there is a serious problem.

Yu. "Which problem?"
M. "There is an insufficient number of . . . [various categories of workers]."
Andropov: "And what are the salaries of the machine- operators?"
Chikirev: "They are decent."

[Andropov then addresses himself to the planer, S. A. Korolev.]

Andropov: "Have you been working here for long?"

---

[446] Ibid.

[447] V. Savenko and P. Sedorov, *P,* September 4, 1982.

[448] M. Klepnikov, quoted by A. Chernyak, *P*, November 29, 1982.

[449] V. Vakhnin, *P*, June 1, 1980.

[450] D. Senin, *P*, April 8, 1982. Emphasis added.

[451] L. Okhorzin, *P*, January 26, 1983.

Korolev: "Seven years."
Andropov: "And what do you earn?"
Korolev: "A normal amount."
Andropov: "But precisely what?"
Korolev: "It amounts to 250 rubles."
Andropov: "But a metalworker earns more?"
Korolev: "No, about the same."

[Andropov addresses himself to another worker, M. F. Skripkin.]

Andropov: "Confidentially, one question, how much do you earn?"
Skripkin: "Sufficiently."
Andropov: "How large is your family?"
Skripkin: "We are two."[452]

* * * * * * * *

Party voices, when stressing the immorality of striving for personal income, usually imply the strength of that motive. They do not publicly insist, however, on what they probably perceive to be the weakness of the desire for income in relation to the aversion to work (see above), and hence "the insufficiency of economic means of influence."[453] "True, last year absentees and lovers of drinking during working hours were deprived, in full or in part, of the 13th monthly pay. Nevertheless, even that measure was not at all effective. The number of absentees was only half of that of the first quarter of last year, but the length of absences increased. The amount of work time lost remained about the same."[454] "Often machine-builders prefer paying a forfeit to delivering the full amount to which they have obliged themselves—no efforts are necessary for the former."[455] "The main thing in the success of production activity," one may conclude, "is the creation in people of a mood for work. . . . 'For a person,' says the Secretary of the Party Committee of the enterprise, A. Dragun, 'it is not only . . . the wage which is important. . . . '"[456]

Back, then, to *pod'em* and *dolg*. "The plans . . . of the Party are grandiose; they can be fulfilled only through *selfless* work. . . . "[457]

---

[452]*P*, February 1, 1983.

[453]L. Brezhnev, at the July 1979 plenum, quoted in I. Syroezhin, *K*, 1980, No. 14, p. 42.

[454]V. Kormushin and others, *P*, April 24, 1980.

[455]L. Reznikov, *P*, August 4, 1980.

[456]G. Krivoshein, *PZh*, 1979, No. 16, p. 41.

[457]Editorial, *K*, 1982, No. 2, p. 3. Emphasis added.

"Economic levers and stimuli cannot in full measure secure the attainment of the aim set."[458]

* * * * * * * *

Such half-heartedness toward the income incentive may contribute to the Party top's singular willingness to present the degree of application of that incentive as being beyond its control. "Regrettably . . . there is every kind of excessive equality (*uravnilovka*), the determination of wages . . . merely according to presence at the work place and not according to the . . . results of work, the conferring of unmerited premiums."[459] "One still encounters situations in which it is economically disadvantageous for enterprises and associations to adopt plans calling for strenuous effort to speed up scientific-technical progress, to raise the quality of production. We have not yet succeeded in eliminating indicators that . . . push toward waste."[460] "Until now, *it must be acknowledged,* the progressive forms [of the organization of labor] are being adopted too slowly. For instance, nobody seems to doubt the utility of the Shchekin method. . . . However, until now, only 6 percent of industrial enterprises work in Shchekin fashion."[461] "There would not seem to be any need to demonstrate the advantages of such teams [brigades] to anyone. Yet the team method is being introduced slowly and not always consistently."[462] "The progressive forms of the payment for work spread with insufficient speed. . . . Until now *we have not succeeded in obtaining a turn for the better* in this domain. . . . "[463] Would the Kremlin allow itself to present its power as so limited in a matter about which its preferences were less mixed?

KONTROL'

Communism, it is asserted, is absence of *kontrol'*—that is, of surveillance and correction of one's performance by others. "The Party poses the task of . . . creating self-discipline among workers. . . . 'The very essence of communism is that every citizen has to a high degree . . . the feeling of responsibility to society' [Brezhnev],"[464] which allows for

---

[458]K. Chernenko 1980, p. 345.

[459]M. Suslov, *PZh*, 1981, No. 9, p. 11.

[460]L. Brezhnev, Central Committee plenum, November 16, 1981. *P*, November 17.

[461]Editorial, *P*, October 5, 1982. Emphasis added.

[462]L. Brezhnev, speech, March 16, 1982, FBIS, March 16, p. R-3.

[463]Editorial, *K*, 1982, No. 16, p. 9. Emphasis added.

[464]I. Yunak, *K*, 1973, No. 3, p. 64.

"the absence of *kontrol'* over the amount of work furnished,"[465] a state of affairs anticipated in the slogan, "The workers' conscience is the best controller."[466]

Yet, in the present, given the limits and drawbacks of relying on *pod'em, dolg* and "material stimulation," *kontrol'* is accorded a decisive role in the Party's instrument panel. "*Kontrol'* and once more *kontrol'*!"[467]

Low *kontrol'* will be followed by low performance. "Often . . . because of the absence of due *kontrol'*, good decisions . . . remain unfulfilled";[468] "even the best decision will remain on paper if there is no good *kontrol'* over fulfillment."[469] "For the fact that some . . . workers fulfilled their obligations inaccurately . . . the Party bureau was in substantial measure responsible. . . . It did not accord due attention to the *kontrol'* and check-up on decisions taken. Therefore, some of the . . . good measures turned out to be unimplemented."[470] "Last year . . . in a Party meeting, preparations for the renewal of Party cards were discussed. The secretaries of the shop Party organizations obliged themselves to take a number of educational and organizational measures. However, because of the lack of *kontrol'* by the Party bureau, nobody did anything for a long time."[471] "The District Committee of Blagodarno in the Territory of Stavropol, for instance, last year twice accepted resolutions on communicating the experience of advanced enterprises. . . . But, as the District Committee did not exercise *kontrol'* over the fulfillment of these decisions, the managers of the sovkhoz and kolkhoz practically did nothing to realize the recommendations. . . . "[472] "I recall the sad admission of the director of a big office: 'They adopted seven decisions on the affair in question, all of which turned out to be fruitless.' The real cause of this fruitlessness . . . was the absence of due *kontrol'*."[473]

High performance *may* exist under low *kontrol'*, but not forever. "He was competent in his job and for a long time worked not badly.

---

465 E. Ivanov and F. Medvedev, *K*, 1979, No. 6, p. 28.

466 Editorial, *K*, 1971, No. 14, p. 11.

467 L. Brezhnev, Central Committee plenum, April 17, 1979, Brezhnev 1981a, p. 15.

468 I. Bondarenko, *K*, 1970, No. 11, p. 35.

469 A. Chernyak, *P*, February 19, 1983.

470 F. Kozyrev, *PZh*, 1976, No. 20, p. 47.

471 Ya. Shvydkov, *PZh*, 1973, No. 4, p. 38.

472 Editorial, *PZh*, 1974, No. 6, p. 7.

473 A. Pelshe, *K*, 1981, No. 11, p. 4.

But then, taking advantage of lack of *kontrol'* he began to fulfill his job duties flaccidly."[474]

When performance is low, look for low *kontrol'* as the cause. "The lagging behind of some sectors of the national economy, the non-fulfillment of objectives of plans, the lack of economy, violations of work discipline—all these are in considerable measure results of an unsatisfactory organization of *kontrol'*. . . . "[475] "Why are there [so] many failures . . . in construction in Saratov? The main reason . . . is the insufficiency of Party *kontrol'*."[476] In fact, "violations and defects [in the work of enterprises] are *usual* where ministries and offices but weakly control the realization of a decision."[477] More than that, "the analysis of [the] facts [of gaps in the implementation of decisions] shows that *all* of them are associated with weakness . . . in *kontrol'*."[478] One may then take the causation link between low performance and low *kontrol'* for granted. "The analysis of the causes of many collectives [in a province] lagging behind . . . shows their low discipline in work and technology, the absence of a due sense of responsibility for missions, *in other words*, the weak control over the fulfillment of decisions."[479]

Conversely, when *kontrol'* is high, decisions will be carried through. Taking this connection for granted, one may succinctly speak of "obtaining oneness of word and deed, a high effectiveness of Party *kontrol'*."[480] Or one may recall in so many words that "a well-performed *kontrol'* brings high discipline in fulfillment. . . . "[481] "*Kontrol'* in general, and Party *kontrol'* in particular, possess a dynamism [that ordinary action lacks—NL]; for its aim is the attainment of concrete results. . . . "[482] "The Party group in a sector of the Kharkov factory producing transport machines . . . worked out . . . a plan for saving materials, energy and labor, and for reducing losses. . . . During the whole year the Party Group kept the fulfillment of the . . . plan under *kontrol'*. The result is clear: all objectives were overfulfilled."[483]

Hence the utopia of completeness in performance through perfection is *kontrol'*: "It is a question of creating a system of control in which

[474]E. Kachalovskii, *PZh*, 1981, No. 18, p. 32.

[475]P. Rybalchenko, *PZh*, 1982, No. 8, p. 50.

[476]A. Vorotnikov, *P*, May 22, 1980.

[477]O. Nikitin and V. Struzhkov, *P*, November 28, 1981. Emphasis added.

[478]A. Pelshe, *K*, 1980, No. 2, p. 21. Emphasis added.

[479]L. Sharaev, *P*, December 14, 1982. Emphasis added.

[480]Editorial note, *P*, February 9, 1982.

[481]K. Chernenko 1980, p. 349.

[482]I. Gustov, *PZh*, 1977, No. 9, p. 20.

[483]V. Shcherbitskii, *PZh*, 1975, No. 2, p. 12.

the very concept of 'nonexecution of adopted decisions' would become impossible."[484]

As the degree of *kontrol'* varies, so does that of fulfillment. "Some city and district committees of the Party . . . verified the implementation of Party decisions but feebly. As a result, some enterprises worked unsteadily last year. . . . The Party committees then began to give more attention to the verification of implementation. Definite results have already been obtained. Production to the amount of 31.3 million rubles above the plan was achieved."[485] "It only needed . . . the Party bureau . . . to strengthen *kontrol'* over the activity [of the enterprise] for the number of alterations of finished products immediately to be reduced by a factor of two."[486]

What is implied in such reports of success—that without *fear*, personnel will perform badly—is only rarely suggested and even less declared: "Concrete decisions were adopted. . . . But not all were realized, as . . . verification of their fulfillment was insufficient. The communists only rarely informed themselves about . . . the fulfillment of decisions taken. But this . . . creates *irresponsibility.*"[487] "If a manager is confident that the Party committee does not master the situation, [that it] is not going to expose him and to shame him, he will without fear adopt the cover of 'objective causes' [for low performance]."[488] On the other hand, under *kontrol'* "every manager and specialist knows [that] he will have to account every month for what he has done in the sector of work with which he is entrusted. He knows that if affairs go badly, he will get no pat on the shoulder."[489]

Relief about having found *a* means to ensure implementation may help to subdue dismay over what the need for recourse to *this* means implies. In any case, it is obviously rare to give public expression to "the question: why do we so often recall the importance of *kontrol'* ? Have our cadres . . . lost the feeling of *dolg*. . . ?"[490]

To help suppress this question, one may employ ambiguous words that *suggest* that *kontrol'* is merely a means to strengthen the sense of *dolg*, rather than replacing it as a motive for proper conduct by the never-mentioned *strakh* (fear) of organizational consequences, of disciplinary sanctions. "Consider our effective methods of *kontrol'*. In such conditions it is practically impossible not to work conscientiously (*po*

---

[484]Unsigned article, *PZh*, 1982, No. 17.

[485]B. Kachura, *PZh*, 1979, No. 16, pp. 17–18.

[486]A. Zolin, *P*, November 28, 1981.

[487]Editorial, *PZh*, 1980, No. 6, p. 28. Emphasis added.

[488]M. Poltoranin and D. Shnyukas, *P*, July 20, 1981.

[489]L. Kretskov, *P*, December 7, 1982.

[490]V. Vorotnikov, *PZh*, 1975, No. 14, p. 14.

sovesti)."[491] *Po sovesti* suggests working *from* conscience, but might, stretching things a bit, also designate working from fear *as* conscience would command. Similarly when *kontrol'* is destined "to *heighten the sense of responsibility* of all officials:"[493] it is suggested that *kontrol'* strengthens conscience, but it could also merely be that *kontrol'* achieves by fear what conscience should, but would not, have accomplished. "The manager lost the feeling of responsibility because the Party organization of the Trust exercised *kontrol'* badly over the actions of management."[494] Did the absence of fear weaken conscience, or did it merely remove the only obstacle to conduct contrary to an always feeble conscience?

Sometimes it is clearly implied or even declared that the point of *kontrol'* is to develop conscience. "Education by *kontrol'*," a headline may proclaim.[495] "*Kontrol'* is one of the most efficient means for educating personnel."[496] "*Kontrol'* educates the cadres in the spirit of high responsibility for their mission."[497] "Experience . . . shows that communists . . . develop ideals and moral qualities more quickly in those primary Party organizations where an effective *kontrol'* over their . . . activities is established. . . . "[498] If this were true, the required amount of *kontrol'* would steadily decline throughout the career of any given target: a clear implication that is never drawn. Hence, statements about the favorable impact of *kontrol'* on conscience seem to be destined rather to veil an enduring defect than to show a path toward its removal.

The pressing problem with *kontrol'* for the Party's top is, in any case, not what this tool reveals about those so much in need of it, but rather the disposition to use the tool insufficiently, if not to misuse it. "In our Party one sometimes meets . . ., on the one hand, an acknowledgment of the importance of *kontrol'*, and, on the other hand—when it comes to doing—an underestimation or even an ignoring of it."[499] "*Kontrol'* of fulfillment remains a weak point in the work of a significant number of Party organizations."[500]

---

[492]A manager, quoted by V. Shalgunov, *P*, December 4, 1981.

[493]L. Brezhnev, at a session of the Presidium of the Supreme Soviet, March 4, 1980, Brezhnev 1981a, p. 292. Emphasis added.

[494]Editorial, *PZh*, 1979, No. 21, p. 7.

[495]*P*, August, 25, 1981.

[496]I. Kapitonov, *PZh*, 1980, No. 14, p. 21.

[497]L. Brezhnev, at the November 1978 plenum, quoted in an unsigned article, *PZh*, 1979, No. 10, p. 57.

[498]F. Kozyrev, *PZh*, 1980, No. 2, p. 47.

[499]A. Pelshe, *K*, 1981, No. 11, p. 4.

[500]M. Suslov, *PZh*, 1981, No. 8, p. 14.

> Equipping the synthetic rubber factory in Yaroslav with new technology proceeded very slowly. . . . Why? The Deputy Minister of Construction, S. E. Yakubanets, the First Deputy Minister of Special Constructions, V. I. Yarmush, and the Deputy Minister for the Petrol-Transforming and Petrochemical Industry, O. G. Murabyan, who had been charged with constantly surveilling the course of fulfillment of the decision taken, did not organize a reliable *kontrol'*. They were not exacting even in those cases where executive discipline had evidently been neglected.[501]

Specifically, "persons called upon to control implementation were frequently working only *formally*."[502] "Certain personnel, instead of properly investigating progress in implementing decisions . . . offering assistance and where necessary calling people . . . to account, confine themselves to fleeting visits, passing remarks, and admonitions. . . . "[503] Control may be intended merely "for show".[504] Thus controllers may fall prey to the penchant for controlling pseudo-activity.

"I always experience a feeling of protest when the bureau *takes* this or that decision *off kontrol'*. I know that not everything that has been planned has been realized, simply [that] the time allotted has come to an end."[505]

"It happens that a real verification of the situation . . . is begun only *when failure* in work *is already evident*, or [a] gross lack of discipline, or serious violations of other moral norms."[506]

The vices of those to be controlled may, as already noted, appear among the controllers: "There are groups and even committees of People's Control which are not distinguished by particular activeness, which prefer living quietly side by side with defects."[507] "A problem . . . preoccupies us: how to raise the sense of responsibility of the members of the commission [for the control of management]?"[508]

Then it becomes a task of any level of the Party to exercise *kontrol'* over the exercise of *kontrol'* by lower levels; even to check up, in a *kontrol'* of the third order, on that of the second. "The Revision

---

[501]Ibid.

[502]V. Shcherbitskii, at a plenum of the Central Committee of the Ukranian Party, November 29, 1982, FBIS, December 14, p. R-20. Emphasis added.

[503]Unsigned article, *K*, 1982, No. 13, FBIS, October 12, 1982, p. 5.

[504]A. Pelshe, *K*, 1981, No. 11, p. 4.

[505]E. Mitrin, *P*, August 3, 1982. Emphasis added.

[506]L. Sharaev, *P*, December 14, 1982. Emphasis added.

[507]V. Klyuev, *P*, October 12, 1982.

[508]E. Sedoi, *PZh*, 1982, No. 11, p. 51.

Committee actually did nothing . . . and the Party Committee did not demand . . . the fulfillment of the mission with which it was charged."[509]

Discouraged by *kontrol'*, one may turn to the idea of relying on *dolg*. "We have many different forms of *kontrol'*," muses a secretary of a Party district committee. "But sometimes we forget about the main *kontroler*: our conscience." In fact, "we should pay more attention to develop . . . such qualities as decency, honesty, a conscientious attitude toward one's job." For "if these are present, we won't need other forms of *kontrol'*."[510] Alas, it is precisely because it seems hopeless to produce these qualities that the "other forms," inefficient as they may be, appear unavoidable.

---

[509]V. Savenko and P. Sedorov, *P*, September 4, 1982.

[510]E. Ugolnik, *P*, June 28, 1982.

Chapter II

NOT GOING TO THE END (*BROSIT' NA POLPUTI*)

The Party's top seems to expect that at levels below it an operation begun will, all too often, not be completed. "Sometimes," one writes, recalling an apparently familiar type of event, "the city committees [of the Party in a province capital] and the province committee stop halfway."[1] "With this," one may observe about some phase of an undertaking, "everything came to an end."[2]

So little may those in charge be attached to completing a task entrusted to them, and so strong may be the penchant "to present"—not only to others, but also to oneself—"what has not been done as accomplished,"[3] that they may believe they have fulfilled their mission when they have not. "In a number of cases, when we considered in the Party bureau the question of taking this or that decision off *kontrol'*, it turned out that it had not been fulfilled. . . . "[4]

Stikhiia [spontaneity], and *samotek* [the drift of events left to themselves] incline one toward noncompletion. As to changes in the "economic mechanism" already decided by the top, "if the interbranch commission of the Gosplan and its section on the perfecting of planning will set their hope only on the ministries, the work will be dragged out over many years and may even stop halfway."[5] Indeed, "all of us often come to a stop halfway."[6]

For completion to occur, a high countereffort is necessary. "All this," one may conclude, "allows making sure that operations begun will be conducted to their end."[7]

"To lead an operation begun to its end" requires an urge and a "skill"[8] which can be called excellence. "Not a few examples can be cited where what was intended was brought to completion."[9] "Take the communist, N. Kirilov. In case he undertakes something, then he

---

[1]V. Katanev, *P*, July 14, 1980.

[2]L. Gorbachev, *PZh*, 1979, No. 17, p. 76.

[3]A. Medyanin, *P*, May 10, 1982.

[4]A. Kostenko, *PZh*, 1972, No. 7, p. 41.

[5]Editorial, *P*, February 15, 1982.

[6]A secretary of a Party city committee quoted in *P*, January 16, 1983.

[7]Editorial, *PZh*, 1981, No. 21, p. 5.

[8]A manager, quoted in *PZh*, 1980, No. 23, p. 54.

[9]Editorial, *P*, June 9, 1981.

assuredly brings it to an end."[10] "The experience of the Party organization [in the Ukraine] provides a number of convincing examples of their heightened ability not only to formulate a plan of action, but to implement it."[11] In fact, there "the work of most Party committees is characterized by the aspiration to complete projects. . . . This has become a characteristic feature of their daily activities."[12] "All of them [candidates for a position] . . . recommended themselves as principled Party people, capable of . . . "—a Westerner might not expect what follows—" . . . leading an operation that has been begun to its end."[13] Even "the authority of a newspaper is to a large extent determined by the ability of the editors to lead an operation begun to its end."[14] And "the ability to bring what has been started to a conclusion is the main quality of the Party leader."[15] "I remember no case," it is said about a model cadre, "in which he would throw away [*brosit'*] halfway what he had begun."[16] And here is the end of a portrait of a first secretary of a district committee: "One could tell much more about the style of work of our district committee and its first secretary. He would deserve that. I will only single out what is in my view the main thing: Whatever affair Shukshin undertakes, he makes the effort to lead it to its end."[17]

So strong is the inclination not to complete that it may appear worthwhile to describe the sequence of phases in a type of operation from start to finish:

> Practical experience confirms that ensuring the unity of word and action . . . begins at the stage of . . . the sober assessment of reality. Subsequently, it becomes more important to . . . formulate clear and substantiated . . . tasks. However, this, too, is insufficient. Proper plans for their implementation must be elaborated. . . . Available material and manpower resources must be assessed, and means for their most effective utilization found. Naturally, it is necessary to . . . determine the personal responsibility of individuals, and develop effective *kontrol'* of execution.[18]

One may stress the advantages from implementing a decision rather than leaving it unrealized: "Decisions are adopted for the purpose of

---

[10]N. Zlobin, *PZh*, 1980, No. 5, p. 19.

[11]V. Shcherbitskii, speech, 1980, *K*, No. 6, April 1980, p. 18.

[12]Loc. cit., p. 21.

[13]V. Burov, *PZh*, 1981, No. 8, p. 57.

[14]Editorial, *P*, January 20, 1982.

[15]E. Shevardnadze, *Zarya Vostoka*, June 5, 1982, FBIS, July 9, p. R-42.

[16]E. Muravyev, *P*, August 12, 1982.

[17]M. Romanenko, *P*, February 6, 1983.

[18]V. Shcherbitskii, speech, 1980, *K*, No. 8, April 1980, p. 18.

realizing them."[19] When "the law is transformed into life, that brings good results."[20] Last but not least, "conducting to the end what has been begun heightens the authority of the communists . . . "[21]—special people capable of such a feat.

Hence, "it is time . . . that we carry every useful operation to the end."[22] "If you begin towing, tow until the end."[23] "The chief aim [in construction] is the delivery of a fully completed building."[24]

* * * * * * * *

"Generosity in promises and avarice in action"[25] seems to be a familiar, if deplorable, combination. "There are persons who easily assume any obligations, but do not fulfill them." "It happens that a manager has recourse to an easy way of conquering authority. Not taking account of real possibilities, he promises to give somebody an apartment almost tomorrow, to another a place for a child in the kindergarten, to a third a sojourn in a sanitarium. But when the time indicated for the fulfillment of the promise arrives, he spreads his arms (*rukami razvodit'*): ' . . . alas, excuse me, you will have to be patient.'"[26] "The managers of many collective and Soviet farms, inviting the young to remain in them, do not spare promises. And then they forget them."[27] "There are those who boast with big numbers, trumpet about their objectives . . . but then quickly forget them."[28] "Some Party organizations are interested only in one thing, to attribute as many missions as possible to communists, to have them put forward (on paper) ever new initiatives. . . . What the effectiveness of this is becomes a matter of the tenth order."[29] "Sometimes one is astonished about the ease with which directors of construction enterprises . . . name dates for the delivery of objects and . . . [ellipses in the text—NL] violate them."[30] During the difficult winter of 1978–1979 in Leningrad, "the methods of leadership bore in part a declaratory character. There was no avarice

---

[19] V. Vasilets, *P*, October 3, 1980.

[20] I. Kapitonov, *K*, 1976, No. 11, p. 39.

[21] G. Shapoval, *PZh*, 1978, No. 12, p. 49.

[22] L. Brezhnev, quoted in *K*, 1979, No. 11, p. 46.

[23] Quoted in V. Grishin, speech, September 25, 1978, Grishin 1979, pp. 533–547.

[24] Editorial, *P*, October 9, 1980.

[25] M. Suslov, *PZh*, 1979, No. 21, p. 18.

[26] Editorial, *P*, April 4, 1982.

[27] Editorial, *P*, January 12, 1982.

[28] Editorial, *P*, February 3, 1980.

[29] A. Margovenko, *P*, March 5, 1982.

[30] G. Krivyakov, *P*, February 15, 1981.

with regard to promises, but the deed did not always follow upon the word."[31]

It is not likely to do so even when the promise is made in response to seemingly serious pressure. "A person beats his breast in public, accepts criticism, affirms that he will do everything as it should be done." [He will say, for example, "allow me to assure you," which furnishes the headline for an article describing such conduct in *Pravda*, January 30, 1983—NL.] "Then he leaves the rostrum and forgets his promise."[32] "The director, N. E. Popov, and the chief engineer, V. G. Gofman, limited themselves to a public acknowledgment of their mistakes . . . and asserted that they would not spare forces so as to correct them. But in fact, they drew no conclusions [from the criticism directed at them], continued to work as before."[33]

> In October [1979] . . . the Bureau of the Central Committee of the CP of Belorussia examined . . . the unsatisfactory progress in construction. Ministers Comrades M. I. Mozolyako and I. A. Antonovich gave assurances that they would take the necessary steps for the . . . fulfillment of plan targets. Two months have passed since that day. But no . . . changes can be observed.[34]

This is "the practice of some individual leaders who promise that the task set will be accomplished in time; who commit themselves before colleagues to eradicate shortcomings and so forth. Having promised and committed themselves, they do not keep their word; do not do anything and do not eradicate. Yet they do not feel embarrassed to shake hands with the others. They report on their failure without blushing; do not feel ashamed while giving accounts."[35]

A promise may be made and broken more than once. "Comrade Medvedev promised that he would reform, but no acts followed his words. . . . He did not come to Party meetings. After each absence we talked with him, and every time he . . . affirmed that he would not commit any violations of Party discipline anymore. However, he continued to conduct himself as before."[36] "During the last years there was not a Party meeting in which they [managers] were not criticized. . . . Each time they recognized their mistakes and promised . . . to remove

---

[31]G. Smaglienko, *PZh*, 1979, No. 5, p. 42.

[32]I. Kudinov, *P*, April 15, 1981.

[33]F. Kuzbaev, *PZh*, 1972, No. 4, p. 52.

[34]P. Masherov, speech, USSR Report: Political and Sociological Affairs, JPRS 76088, pp. 133–148.

[35]V. Shcherbitskii, speech at the Donetsk Province Committee plenum, October 29, 1982, FBIS, November 5, 1982, p. R-3.

[36]Unsigned article, *PZh*, 1979, No. 17, p. 75.

the defects. However, the deed does not always follow the word."[37] "In many institutions the practice of . . . promising and then not fulfilling disappears but slowly. When one term has expired, another one is put forward—and this several times."[38]

Such habits imply widespread complicity with those who default on their promises—a point not missed by the Kremlin. "Nobody asks Boyarshimov why his promises had turned out to be empty sounds."[39] Usually, obligations [in socialist competition] are enunciated from the height of the speaker's platform under applause. And those who did not keep their word? Why not ask them to account for their work before the collective . . . ?"[40]

In such conditions it becomes appropriate to insist on the principle that promises should be kept. "As I understand it," one may say at the end of a distressing tale, "all recipes [on the issue at hand] amount to one thing: one must keep one's word under any circumstances."[41] "If you have given your word, keep it; if you have promised it, do it."[42] "Let us follow the fundamental rule: *If you make a promise, keep it. If a pledge is adopted, fulfill it!*"[43]

To behave properly in this respect is a point of excellence. "V. M. Pismennii . . . is famous in the factory . . . as a man of his word. If he gives a promise, he surely fulfills it."[44] But this is rare; hence "it is particularly important to develop in all workers the capacity to keep a given word."[45] Under the headline, "A Person Who Takes His Duty Seriously," he is said to be "like a stone wall. He does not leave [one] in a lurch; he fulfills what he has promised in good time."[46]

* * * * * * * *

An operation may not be completed because of an always-to-be-expected falling-off of the *aktivnost'* of those engaged in it (see above). "We undertake an operation energetically, and then we give it

---

[37]V. Shevchuk, *PZh*, 1981, No. 17, p. 41.

[38]V. Kuznetsov, *K*, 1980, No. 16, p. 21.

[39]V. Gryzan, *P*, January 30, 1983.

[40]L. Gorshkov, *P*, February 19, 1983.

[41]A. Kolesnikov, *P*, August 29, 1980.

[42]*PZh*, 1972, No. 14, p. 63.

[43]G. Romanov, speech, January 14, 1982, *Leningradskaya Pravda*, January 15. FBIS, January 28, p. R-17. Emphasis in the original.

[44]V. Burkov, *PZh*, 1975, No. 11, p. 46.

[45]Editorial, *K*, 1980, No. 9, p. 6.

[46]Editorial, *P*, April 4, 1982.

up [*brosit'*—literally, throw away] halfway"[47]—perhaps in a "thoughtless renunciation of well-founded decisions taken earlier."[48] "In one place [in construction in Saratov Province] they began construction projects and then gave up."[49] "The directing body . . . did not show perseverance with regard to the completion of many good undertakings."[50]

What has been begun may be forgotten rather than completed: "The person himself forgets the mission with which he has been charged";[51] "The Party bureau . . . forgot its decision."[52] "At the beginning of the Five-Year Plan, Aleksandr Fedorovich [a metal worker] obligated himself to fulfill seven yearly tasks in five years. It seemed that his initiative was approved and supported. There were slogans, special issues of the factory news bulletin. And then slowly everything was forgotten."[53] "Remember what happened to the milling-machine operator, S. Vodkov, when he decided to work according to the method of the innovator-turner, Albert Pavlov. First he was supported . . . and then they forgot about the new method of work. Now the milling-machine operator Vodkov again works in the old fashion."[54] This is what is going to happen unless the Party "sustains the required tonus in . . . fulfillment."[55]

Those conducting an operation may underestimate the energy and the time it requires and end it too soon—a penchant that the leadership may combat by recalling that any important objective is apt to take a long time and much work to attain. "The restructuring of ideological activity is not a campaign of short duration, but a many-faceted and painstaking effort lasting years."[56]

In these conditions the Party's top insists on insisting—that is, on exercising "Bolshevik stubbornness in attaining objectives."[57] "A political line is established only when one struggles to obtain a set objective day after day, month after month, not renouncing one's word, not for-

---

[47]N. Duboshin, *P*, April 25, 1981.

[48]N. Tikhonov, *K*, 1979, No. 7, p. 38.

[49]A. Vorotnikov, *P*, May 22, 1980.

[50]V. Shangin, *PZh*, 1981, No. 3, p. 64.

[51]Yu. Bashkatov, *P*, March 14, 1982.

[52]E. Bratolyubov, *P*, June 9, 1980.

[53]Ibid.

[54]E. Fakov, *PZh*, 1971, No. 23, p. 37.

[55]A. Pelshe, *K*, 1980, No. 2, p. 22.

[56]Unsigned article, *K*, 1982, No. 1, p. 23.

[57]V. Lomakin, *PZh*, 1980, No. 16, p. 27.

getting one's resolutions."[58] "What did I learn from him? Stubbornness in the obtaining of an aim. . . . "[59] "This did not succeed immediately, but he turned out to be a stubborn person . . . [ellipsis in the original—NL]."[60]

Not abandoning an enterprise one has begun is praiseworthy. "Whatever happens, he does not throw away [*brosit'*] what he has begun."[61] "Ten years were required from each of the researchers for their . . . great search. Somebody asked: are we not going to falter, are we not going to get tired? They did not get tired, they did not falter . . . [ellipsis in the original—NL]." [62] "We communists are persevering. We entered on this path and we shall not leave it."[63] "From my mother," Brezhnev discloses, "I adopted stubbornness, patience, a habit of absolutely conducting an operation to its end, once I had undertaken it."[64]

* * * * * * * *

An operation, the Party's leadership observes with concern, may be abandoned in the face of difficulty, when "any difficulty encountered is affirmed to be insurmountable."[65]

The "ability not to retreat before difficulties"[66] is a mark of excellence. "But they do not get dispirited, they do not give up."[67]

* * * * * * * *

Or an undertaking may be left incomplete, as one shifts to another that may later suffer the same fate. At first "we support . . . an initiative, but then other worries and affairs obscure it, the attention to it . . . weakens."[68] "A manager seizes now one operation and now another, and often does not carry either one to the end."[69] In Donets Province, "though several thousand constructions were still in process,

[58]L. Brezhnev, *Vozrozhdenie*, Brezhnev 1979, p. 71.

[59]A. Pozdnyakov, *P*, October 16, 1980.

[60]V. Liventsov, *P*, July 4, 1982.

[61]N. Pivovarov, *P*, December 31, 1981.

[62]A. Starukhin, *P*, February 4, 1982.

[63]L. Brezhnev, speech at the 26th Party Congress, February 23, 1981. Brezhnev 1981a, p. 675.

[64]L. Brezhnev 1981b, p. 10.

[65]G. Krivoshein, *PZh*, 1978, No. 2, p. 18.

[66]A. Khudyak, *PZh*, 1978, No. 1, p. 65.

[67]F. Kozyrev, *PZh*, 1980, No. 2, p. 46.

[68]N. Kirichenko, *P*, May 26, 1980.

[69]G. Shilyaev, *PZh*, 1979, No. 1, p. 30.

in 1977 some [1500] new ones were begun."[70] To begin attracts, to complete or to modify repels. While "as a rule it is economically advantageous to obtain an increase in production by . . . the modernization of an enterprise," an "excessive fraction of resources is directed toward new construction."[71] Hence, "in reviewing the plan for the 1980s, it was proposed to reduce the number of construction projects and to [go all out] for the completion of projects close to being finished,"[72] At a conference it has to be "underscored" that "it is indispensable to direct capital investment in the first place . . . to the completion of constructions begun."[73]

> In 1979 in Sverdlovsk Province at the initiative of the Komsomol . . . there began a competition to save an amount of electrical energy which would be equal to that delivered during a year by a whole *GES* [hydroelectric station]. . . . The count of this *KES* [Komsomol Electric Station] quickly rose. But then its growth slowed up. The cause was the appearance of indifference toward this movement in the city and province committee of the Komsomol and in Party bodies. The new 11th Five-Year Plan was beginning, and they wanted to mark it by some new initiative. . . . They forgot about the "old" one.[74]

* * * * * * * *

An operation may halt in the course of discussing it. "The operation did not proceed beyond words."[75] "Some act according to the principle 'They made a noise and forgot (*poshumeli i zabyli*).'"[76] "Organizational activity . . . often . . . transforms itself into fruitless conversations."[77] "We talk much and do little."[78] "Sometimes one talks for years about the same defects, but no practical measures for their removal are being adopted. . . . "[79] "Hence, it is always appropriate to ask, 'but which trace did the discussion of this question leave?'"[80] "Local Party organizations are often carried away by meetings. . . . Lenin called for a

---

[70]Editorial, *K*, 1978, No. 18, p. 11.

[71]L. Brezhnev, speech at the 24th Party Congress, March 30, 1971. Brezhnev 1972, p. 264.

[72]L. Brezhnev, at the Central Committee plenum, November 27, 1979, Brezhnev 1981a, p. 203.

[73]V. Shangin, *PZh*, 1981, No. 3, p. 63.

[74]A. Margovenko, *P*, March 5, 1982.

[75]L. Skripnikov, *PZh*, 1979, No. 1, p. 46.

[76]Editorial, *P*, February 1, 1983.

[77]V. Shcherbitskii 1978, p. 132.

[78]A foreman, quoted by S. Elizarenko, *PZh*, 1973, No. 21, p. 60.

[79]I. Kapitonov, *K*, 1976, No. 11, p. 36.

[80]Yu. Zhigailov, *P*, October 10, 1980.

struggle against bustle in meetings. The Party is still guided by this,"[81] fighting "the endless consideration of obvious questions."[82] "There should be less talk about improving things and more work. . . . "[83]

The words being spoken may not even specifically refer to the operation being ostensibly prepared. "Businesslike measures are replaced by empty talk."[84] "Chatter flowers . . . chattering. . . . "[85]

It is then up to the Party to "confer upon discussion an aim-directed character . . ., to act so that discussions favor the rise of economic activity."[86]

But actions may not follow upon words. "Everything said is correct, but sometimes the matter does not go further."[87] "These days hundreds of seminars . . . of scientific-practical conferences are being conducted everywhere. But sometimes this happens: they talked, they left, and they forgot."[88] "Not a few seminars and scientific-practical conferences are being conducted, but the . . . yield from them is often not very visible. They came, conversed, returned—that is all. There is no urge to assimilate what has been seen."[89]

Words themselves may become output. "Party organizations sometimes consider meetings . . . almost as the chief criterion of productive work."[90] "Since the 25th Congress of the CPSU, the Bureau of the City Committee and of the District Committee of the Party have heard accounts from 39 managers of industry and of other enterprises and organizations. During the last year all links of the City Party organizations have considered accounts of . . . more than a thousand managers of all categories and activities"—statements of fact followed by remarks in anticipation of an objection: "However, the point is, of course, not to run after a large number of accounts."[91]

For "some managers are unable to go from consideration of defects to . . . actions designed to eliminate them."[92]

In fact, talking may impede acting: "Some members of the Party drown in words. They have little energy left . . . for work. Instead of

---

[81]A. Bodolazskii, *K*, 1979, No. 12, p. 49.

[82]K. Chernenko 1980, p. 200.

[83]Editorial, *P*, March 1, 1982.

[84]M. Suslov, *K*, 1979, No. 15, p. 33.

[85]A. Rybakov, *PZh*, 1980, No. 12, pp. 33–34.

[86]L. Brezhnev, quoted by Yu. Storozhilov, *PZh*, 1981, No. 2, p. 49.

[87]V. Legostaev, *PZh*, 1980, No. 17, p. 52.

[88]Editorial, *P*, March 12, 1980.

[89]P. Masherov, *P*, June 15, 1980.

[90]A. Bodolazskii, *K*, 1979, No. 12, p. 49.

[91]V. Sakalauskas, *PZh*, 1980, No. 16, p. 42.

[92]M. Suslov, *PZh*, 1979, No. 21, p. 16.

rolling up their shirtsleeves and beginning to work, they agitate each other for a long time [with] 'consider the question.'"[93]

Hence, "it would be good to have fewer words and more action."[94] Hence, the stress on "the ability to firmly link words with actions,"[95] "the principle: from analysis to action,"[96] "an orientation toward accomplishments rather than loud words."[97] For "you understand"—or rather, you do not—"that in politics not only words are needed."[98] "Deserving of . . . support are those farms where they have shifted from talking about protein to specific deeds. . . . "[99] "Today the slogan, *act!* [emphasis in the original—NL], must be the . . . combat slogan for all the agroindustrial complex personnel. The Party has formulated a good . . . program, and the main thing now is not to engage in idle talk, but precisely to act."[100]

For, as noted earlier, "there are those who will not fail to use any possibility for pronouncing a sonorous speech. But when it comes to acting, they disappear into the dark."[101] While "passionate speeches" are pronounced, "little businesslike activity goes on"[102]—a combination whose frequency of occurrence provokes an insistence on "the ability to arrange . . . work without noise."[103] "Cadres limit themselves to abstract considerations 'concerning the existing defects,' remain prisoners of general phrases, not connecting words with deeds."[104]

"You know," one may observe, "it is possible to repeat indefatigably the same *appeals* without affairs moving from place"[105]—which might also be said about this very sentence, given prominence by Andropov upon his accession. "They indicate a task, and speak and speak of it, undertaking little for its accomplishment."[106] "Work on . . . economy of material resources often amounts to nothing more than appeals."[107]

---

[93]V. Lebedeva, *P*, January 14, 1982.

[94]A worker quoted in *P*, February 1, 1983.

[95]V. Shcherbitskii, speech, *K*, No. 6, April 1980, p. 31.

[96]Editorial, *P*, January 25, 1980.

[97]Yu. Andropov, speech, December 21, 1982. *P*, December 22.

[98]L. Brezhnev, speech, October 27, 1982. *P*, October 28.

[99]M. Gorbachev, speech, *K*, No. 11, August 1980, pp. 36–49.

[100]V. Golikov, *K*, 1982, No. 13, FBIS, September 28, Annex, p. 2.

[101]V. Grishin, *PZh*, 1972, No. 1, p. 16.

[102]G. Shilyaev, *PZh*, 1979, No. 1, p. 31.

[103]V. Konotop, *PZh*, 1977, No. 6, p. 27.

[104]M. Suslov, *PZh*, 1979, No. 21, p. 23.

[105]S. Toporkov, *PZh*, June 28, 1980. Emphasis added.

[106]V. Lebedeva, *P*, June 14, 1982.

[107]G. Romanov, at the plenum of the Leningrad Province Committee, December 3, 1982, *Leningradskaya Pravda*, December 4, FBIS, December 20, p. R-18.

"There is much talk about increasing efficiency and quality, but . . . little real movement."[108] "Sometimes this happens: in the factory . . . there is uninterrupted talk about the necessity of a scientific organization of work. But there is no increase in the productivity of labor, the quality of products does not improve."[109] Seven years later the author copies his passage.[110]

Words rejecting inaction, *calling for action*, replace action. Cadres then "declare that it is indefensible not to begin to act. But as soon as the time for action has come, they manage to remain somewhere on the side. . . . "[111]

One may be impelled not to act on "appeals" by reason of their stark contrast with reality: "After a lecture on economy, people see rusting metal and thrown-away machine tools in the factory courtyard. . . . "[112] Hence, the requirement: "and not only words about discipline, not only appeals to order."[113]

Limiting oneself to "appeals" may be fostered by attributing overmuch power to them, a belief that then needs to be rejected: "The most passionate discourses on exactingness and personal responsibility cannot replace real exactingness and effective demandingness."[114] "It is possible to talk endlessly about the necessity of heightening exactingness. . . . But if words are not backed by deeds, nothing will result."[115]

* * * * * * * *

When an undertaking extends beyond analysis and appeal, it may yet stop with a decision. There are "managers [who] spend most of their time composing . . . resolutions, not thinking about when and with what forces they could be fulfilled."[116] "In the style of work of some organizations the following sequence has taken roots: the preparation of . . . a meeting, which absorbs the main forces of the apparatus; the meeting with a report of the leading worker, and, naturally, with a discussion lasting many hours; the adoption of a resolution . . . asking a lower level to begin an operation. . . . Before all this reaches the lower level, another question for a meeting has

---

[108] A. Smirnov, *PZh*, 1978, No. 8, p. 32.
[109] G. Krivoshein, *K*, 1971, No. 18, p. 37.
[110] *PZh*, 1978, No. 2, p. 20.
[111] Editorial, *PZh*, 1978, No. 13, p. 7.
[112] M. Suslov, *PZh*, 1979, No. 21, p. 18.
[113] G. Belov, *PZh*, 1980, No. 6, p. 48.
[114] V. Legostaev, *PZh*, 1980, No. 5, p. 40.
[115] A. Pelshe, *K*, 1980, No. 2, p. 25.
[116] I. Klinenko, *PZh*, 1974, No. 20, p. 22.

already matured—everybody is busy again."[117] "Sometimes this happens: a question is prepared, the wheel of organizational work is turning at full speed—commissions are created, accounts are established, forces are distributed. When the operation has reached the stage of fulfilling the decision taken, steam should be added, but precisely then it is reduced—often not because staff is lacking, but rather because it is then already diverted to the preparation of another document."[118] "There are many cases where . . . nothing has been done on behalf of a decision at the moment, when the next has already been adopted."[119]

Once a decision is taken, it may be forgotten. "Every time pretty good decisions were adopted, and every time they were immediately forgotten."[120] "How did the Party organizations of the shops and the Party bureau react to an unfavorable situation? They assembled, they discussed the situation, they disapproved of the negligent ones, they adopted appropriate decisions, they put the protocols into the proper file cabinets, and the situation remained as before."[121]

When those who take a decision promptly forget about it, they forget that those charged with executing it are in turn apt to forget about the duty (Chap. I). "The members of the Party meeting . . . obliged the newly elected bureau to take measures so as to remove the existing defects. But what did the Party Bureau, headed by F. Malikov, do? Nothing. The secretary shrugged his shoulders: We forgot."[122]

"Often we consider a certain question once more, not in order to introduce something new, but because the situation . . . has not changed," although "it would be more correct first to ask those charged with executing the decision already taken why they have not done so."[123] "Indeed, it *should* become the rule that any new decision on the same question be taken only after past decisions have been fulfilled and new circumstances have emerged."[124] Yet, "the state of affairs in . . . has been considered more than once by the Province Committee, which has taken detailed decisions. But the situation has changed little."[125] "Sometimes, when a decision has turned out to be unfulfilled, a second and sometimes even a third decision on the same question is

---

[117]A. Pelshe, *K*, 1981, No. 11, p. 11.

[118]N. Umanets, *P*, July 3, 1981.

[119]L. Kletskov, *PZh*, 1983, No. 8, p. 34.

[120]E. Fakov, *PZh*, 1971, No. 23, p. 36.

[121]Unsigned article, *PZh*, 1975, No. 21, p. 30.

[122]A. Petrushov, *P*, July 21, 1981.

[123]F. Kulikov, *P*, January 16, 1982.

[124]Yu. Andropov, Central Committee plenum, November 22, 1982, FBIS, November 23, p. R-3. Emphasis added.

[125]Editorial, *P*, October 10, 1980.

taken."[126] Thus "decisions . . . often copy others that have already been adopted, but have remained unfulfilled."[127] It is then a matter of "duplicating decisions with the time allowed for execution brought forward."[128] "Time passed, new orders followed the old ones, but as before, there was no improvement."[129] "All the points of the project of resolution submitted to the Party meeting . . . had migrated word for word from the protocol of last year's meeting, which in turn was hardly different from that of the previous year."[130]

> Five years ago the bureau of the Priluk City Committee considered the question of increasing the effectiveness of production and the quality of the products of the factory Zhivmash. Serious omissions in the work of the Party organization and management were uncovered, measures for improvement indicated. After some time, the bureau again heard the Party committee of Zhivmash, again noted defects in its work. . . . Again, paths for the removal of these defects were indicated. . . . However, in 1980 the City Committee returned again to the question and the next resolution was born.[131]

"In the bureau of the Dzerzhinskii District Committee of the Communist Party of the Ukraine . . . during the last year . . . questions concerning the coke-chemical factory in Krivoi Rog were considered seven times. Every time a decision was adopted. However, because of the weak work on the fulfillment of the decision, the situation in the factory did not change."[132] "During 15 months the Province Direction of Agricultural Production sent to various offices more than 10,000 documents in 150,000 copies. A considerable part of these pieces of paper . . . repeated orders, directives, instructions issued before."[133]

Thus, "it happens that the adoption of a decision is preceded by much work by the Party Committee. But as soon as the document is . . . accepted, activity falls, and the matter . . . is left to itself."[134]

Such conduct, the Party's leadership observes, may be accompanied by indifference toward the fate of the decision taken, justified by an appropriate limitation of one's task. "We take the next decision. The section that had prepared the project heaves a sigh of relief: it's over.

[126] L. Brezhnev, at the 25th Party Congress, quoted in *PZh*, 1980, No. 9, p. 44.

[127] A. Pelshe, *K*, 1981, No. 11, p. 11.

[128] I. Gustov, *PZh*, 1977, No. 9, p. 20.

[129] Ibid.

[130] Yu. Zhigailov, *P*, October 10, 1980.

[131] N. Umanets, *P*, July 3, 1981.

[132] Editorial, *PZh*, 1970, No. 22, p. 5.

[133] G. Krivoshein, *PZh*, 1978, No. 2, p. 20.

[134] Editorial, *PZh*, 1976, No. 22, p. 11.

The burden is off the shoulders, the question closed."[135] "The meeting proceeded . . . on a good level. But what happens afterward, how it influenced the situation in a practical way, . . . preoccupies the Party committee only little.[136]

Alternatively, halting at a point of decision is fostered by believing, or pretending to believe, in the power of a decision itself to induce its own implementation—that is, by attributing to subordinates precisely the opposite of what is the case, a high sense of duty (see Chap. I). "They adopted a decision and ceased being concerned with the matter, assuming that from then on the operation would proceed by itself."[137] "The Party Secretary, the Bureau, the Party Committee apparently consider that once a decision has been adopted, operations will proceed by themselves."[138] "The District Committee took two decisions on the same organization in which serious defects in the activity of the Party bureau and its secretary were noted. . . . As if it believed in the magic power of paper, the District Committee continued to issue one decision after the other. . . . "[139]

However, the Party leadership advances—expressing its *general* denial of good things occurring by themselves, but silent about the state of the sense of duty in *particular*: "It is well known that to take a decision is only part of the operation";[140] "One might even say that to take a decision . . . is only a beginning."[141] "It would be wrong to equate what is planned with what has already been done";[142] "It would be wrong to assume that after taking even the best resolutions everything will suddenly . . . change."[143] For "it is well known that even the best decision will remain on paper if a persistent struggle for its realization is not waged."[144] "It is known that no decision, as well taken as it might be, will be . . . fulfilled if it is not strengthened by . . . efforts . . . with regard to its . . . implementers. A decision will have a noticeable impact only if . . . there is concern with its . . . fulfillment on the part of Party and government organs."[145]

---

[135]E. Mitrin, *P*, August 3, 1982.

[136]V. Shirokov, *P*, October 14, 1981.

[137]M. Semenov, *P*, June 2, 1981.

[138]M. Vakharchenko and L. Yarovnikov, *PZh*, 1970, No. 12, p. 46.

[139]G. Kalugin, *PZh*, 1972, No. 14, p. 44.

[140]I. Morozov, *PZh*, 1978, No. 4, p. 24.

[141]Editorial, *P*, July 7, 1981.

[142]K. Chernenko 1980, p. 245.

[143]N. Umantsov, quoted by M. Odinets and A. Chernyak, *P*, August 1, 1982.

[144]F. Loshchenko, *K*, 1970, No. 1, p. 33.

[145]A. Pelshe, *K*, 1980, No. 2, p. 20.

Hence, what we need now is not new decisions, but "above all the fulfillment of what has already been decided;"[146] make it come true that "to decide means to implement!"[147] "Having taken a decision, it is inadmissible to throw the matter away halfway. All that has been decided must be fulfilled."[148] The need is for "people to be concerned . . . that decisions taken do not remain on paper,"[149] rather than "being enticed into adopting *numerous* decisions,"[150] considering a decision as a unit of output, and, by the very fact of multiplying decisions, making it infeasible to fulfill all of them. "One of the causes of the abundance of decisions taken [by Party organs] is, in fact, this: there . . . are people who judge the work of a Party committee according to whether a certain question has been considered at the meeting of the bureau or the plenum. Then everybody tries to provide himself with paper so that he may not be reproached for *inaction*."[151] In clearer (and rare) words: "The abundance of resolutions is sometimes dictated by the wish to have a 'shelter' in case of verification. . . . Look, measures were taken!"[152]

* * * * * * * *

Insensitivity to the proposition that taking a decision should be followed by an implementation action is expressed, so the Party leadership observes, by the disposition not to name implementers in, or in connection with, the decision itself. "The Tyanshansk District Committee in Narynsk Province [of Kirgizia] during the last two years adopted five times resolutions concerning the improvement of measures for the preservation of socialist property. But the benefit from this was small because their decisions were . . . without addresses."[153]

When there are such "addresses," the decision in question may be communicated to them with a delay, or not at all: "Often . . . the decisions adopted by Party committees are sent to Party organizations with much delay; sometimes even after the time which has been specified in these decisions has run out; or they are even never transmitted . . . at all."[154]

---

[146]N. Bolyukh and N. Umanets, *P*, February 15, 1980.

[147]Editorial, *P*, March 2, 1983.

[148]Yu. Andropov, *K*, 1983, No. 3, p. 13.

[149]Editorial, *P*, January 25, 1980.

[150]B. Kenchura, *PZh*, 1979, No. 16, p. 14. Emphasis added.

[151]V. Kiryushkin, *P*, April 15, 1981. Emphasis added.

[152]K. Fomichenko, *P*, July 20, 1980.

[153]K. Fomichenko, *P*, July 20, 1980.

[154]N. Shvats, *PZh*, 1980, No. 9, p. 43.

When those who should execute a decision are named and the decision is communicated to them in good time, it may still not be clear what precisely is demanded: "It often happens that . . . Party organizations adopt documents full of general appeals which . . . because of their indeterminateness . . . oblige nobody to anything whatsoever."[155]

* * * * * * *

Once a decision is taken, a halt may still occur during arrangements for its implementation—which are then not used. "We [in a sovkhoz] decided . . . to reinforce the production of fodder. . . . There was much talk about this decision. All ended with the creation of a new office, that of the assistant director for the production of fodder. For the rest, everything remains the same."[156] "On the surface everything often looks . . . fine. Decisions have been taken . . . about arrangements for *kontrol'*: commissions have been created, inquiries are being prepared, collegial bodies have met. But there is no real improvement."[157] "The necessary steps are, as it were, taken. . . . The appropriate orders are given, the people responsible for fulfillment appointed, the deadlines determined. But that is where the matter ends."[158] "In . . . [one] case, everything necessary seems to have been done: an order is issued, conditions are elaborated. In short, the affair seems to be launched, you only have to wait for results. However, again and again there is no movement."[159]

* * * * * * *

Having entered upon implementing a decision, and having come close to completing the operation, one might still stop short of finishing it, ending work with a *nedodelka*, an imperfect product. "Often residential buildings are delivered with imperfections."[160] "In practical terms, the construction is finished, but because of imperfections, it has not been accepted by the government commission."[161]

Hence the stress on "builders leading a fully completed object to utilization,"[162] on seeing "that the economy receives [from the construction

---

[155]V. Shcherbitskii, *K*, 1980, No. 6, p. 30.

[156]I. Duboshin, *P*, April 25, 1981.

[157]A. Pelshe, *K*, 1980, No. 2, p. 21.

[158]O. Nikitin and V. Struzhkov, *P*, November 28, 1981.

[159]A. Brygin, *K*, 1982, No. 15, p. 70.

[160]V. Grishin, speech, March 28, 1968, Grishin 1979, p. 107.

[161]Editorial, *K*, 1981, No. 1, p. 8.

[162]Editorial, *P*, November 10, 1981.

industry] not symbolic production capacities, but production capacities fully capable of work."[163]

Thus, although actions taken up to a point may have been correct, the undertaking might still fail because of incorrect conduct later. "The discussions of problems in the Party committee proceeded as a rule in sharp and businesslike fashion. This led one to believe that the situation in this or that sector of work was going to change for the better. However, time passed and the situation remained the same. The Party committee forgot about organizational work for the fulfillment of decisions taken."[164] "Good decisions were taken, and with that it all ended."[165] "It is possible to take a businesslike decision, to indicate the time for fulfillment and the persons responsible, and yet the task thus set remains unfulfilled."[166] Progress in an operation does not reduce the ever-present probability that it will not be completed.

* * * * * * * *

Ultimate failure to follow through on a decision may be predetermined from the first. Thus, the inclination to scatter forces (Chap. III) condemns many of the operations already begun to a state of incompletion. "The head of the workshop, Comrade Gorshkov, does not trust the foreman and the advanced workers; he concerns himself with everything, and, as a result, nothing is completed."[167] In construction "there is scattering of investments between a multitude of objects being built at the same time. As a result of this, in 1977 in Belorussia alone the amount of unfinished construction rose by more than 200 million rubles."[168] "The Party committee undertook too many operations at the same time, and naturally lacked forces for conducting them to their ends."[169] "They began work everywhere," Brezhnev comments, recalling the reconstruction of a large factory after the war, "and finished nothing."[170] "The verification of implementation is often . . . rendered difficult by the fact that . . . Party committees adopt . . . a large number of decisions."[171]

The inclination not to complete an action may foster the introduction and maintenance of incentives to scatter, even at the cost of

[163]Editorial, *P*, August 11, 1982.

[164]V. Chernov, *PZh*, 1975, No. 19, p. 40.

[165]A. Trishin, *PZh*, 1980, No. 7, p. 31.

[166]A. Tsarkov, *PZh*, 1972, No. 4, p. 53.

[167]A. Razutkin, *PZh*, 1972, No. 11, p. 53.

[168]Unsigned article, *PZh*, 1978, No. 1, p. 29.

[169]V. Chernov, *PZh*, 1975, No. 19, p. 40.

[170]L. Brezhnev, *Vozrozhdenie*, Brezhnev 1979, p. 64.

[171]N. Shvats, *PZh*, 1980, No. 9, p. 42.

completing. "Why is the completion of constructions so dragged out? The first reason is an economic one. It is advantageous to builders to begin ever new [projects] where there are [early on] many capital-intensive operations, and it is disadvantageous to complete the labor-intensive finishing activities."[172] "The scattering of forces and means over numerous constructions . . . allows the construction organizations to fulfill indicators of volume without having the [plants] begin operations."[173] Hence "[work in construction], beginning with the 11th Five-Year Plan, will be evaluated not by the volume of capital invested, but by objects entering into operation. . . . "[174] Ten five-year plans were needed to abolish—at least on paper—such an incentive not to complete. But upon his accession, Andropov speaks as if nothing had changed: "The scattering of forces and means between a host of [construction] projects should be combated . . . resolutely."[175] A few months later, "the aim set [for construction] . . . can be attained only through concentrating forces and means on completing constructions already begun."[176]

* * * * * * * *

Scattering is one of the several practices by which one can come to disregard the limitations of one's means (Chap. VI). "Practically every director tries to begin construction on as many projects as possible, forgetting to ask whether it will be possible to start operations as scheduled."[177] "When five-year and one-year plans have already been established, some ministries 'force (*probivat'*)' decisions in favor of the expansion of this or that enterprise. In most cases this practice is caused by the effort to obtain supplementary capital investments. . . . No account is taken, as a rule, of the possibilities of construction, which puts planned objects under the threat of remaining unfinished."[178] Weighing one's forces before saying one's word "is a necessary condition for its fulfillment," but "not all make that effort. And this is precisely why they issue promises that they cannot fulfill"—even worse, "they issue them not expecting to fulfill."[179] "In the establishment of plans, the dimensions of construction as well as the number of

---

[172]V. Sebastyanov and N. Utkin, *P*, May 14, 1980.

[173]V. Grishin, speech, January 25, 1979, Grishin 1979, p. 561.

[174]Editorial, *P*, October 9, 1980.

[175]The Central Committee plenum, November 22, 1982, FBIS, November 23, p. R-7.

[176]Editorial, *P*, February 4, 1983.

[177]P. Masherov, speech, "USSR Report: Political and Sociological Affairs," JPRS 76088, pp. 133–148.

[178]G. Romanov, *K*, 1978, No. 18, pp. 20–21.

[179]A. Kolesnikov, *P*, August 29, 1980.

objects to be built are often increased without taking account of real possibilities. As a result, the amount of unfinished construction grows."[180] "With regard to an enterprise to which it is intended to entrust the construction of a new object, ministries rarely ask themselves, 'Will it be feasible, do the forces suffice for it?' Usually, there is . . . only one word: 'It should be done . . . !' Often ministries and offices authorize construction for which the resources to be employed are undocumented. The result is another potentially unfinished object."[181]

---

[180]L. Brezhnev, at the 24th Party Congress, March 30, 1971, Brezhnev 1972, p. 264.
[181]V. Sebastyanov and N. Utkin, *P*, May 14, 1980.

Chapter III

SCATTERING (*RASPYLENIE*)

The Party leadership, as noted earlier, perceives a penchant for "the dispersion of resources among objectives."[1] After decades of fighting against it, "scattering still exists."[2] Thus there is a "scattering of scientific forces,"[3] "the dispersal of scientific forces and means on numerous petty subjects."[4] "Up to now we have not succeeded in stopping the . . . scattering of capital investments among multiple objects."[5] "When in a Party committee, questions shift rapidly as in a kaleidoscope. . . . "[6]

It is a penchant difficult to subdue. "We make an effort," a first secretary of a province committee declares, "not to seize 'twenty different affairs'. . . . "[7]

What is already concentrated may nonetheless become scattered: "the pulling asunder of capital investments, the diverting of labor and materials from important government projects."[8] The inclination to scatter oneself is an unthinking "attempt to encompass everything right away"[9]—an attempt that can have consequences contrary to those intended.

Scattering can be a way of making oneself *small.* "Sometimes, instead of . . . working out this or that big problem, forces are being scattered on small . . . questions."[10] "When the main theme disappears from view, when the manager wallows in petty details. . . . "[11]

Scattering can mean being *dominated* by events. Then "we do not command events, but rather throw ourselves from one place to the other like incompetent firemen. We put out fires that arise again,

---

[1]A. Mendeleev, *PZh,* 1981, No. 2, p. 42.

[2]K. Chernenko 1980, p. 220.

[3]Unsigned article, *PZh,* 1975, No. 3, p. 22.

[4]V. Grishin, speech, June 30, 1982, FBIS, July 29, p. U-8.

[5]Editorial, *K,* 1978, No. 18, p. 10; repeating L. Brezhnev at a Central Committee plenum, November 27, 1978. Brezhnev 1979, p. 531.

[6]V. Shubin, *PZh,* 1972, No. 4, p. 55.

[7]V. Klyuev, *P,* September 7, 1981.

[8]L. Brezhnev, at a Central Committee plenum, November 27, 1979, Brezhnev 1981a, p. 203.

[9]Editorial, *P,* October 9, 1982.

[10]K. Bobolyubov, *PZh,* 1981, No. 20, p. 22.

[11]Editorial, *PZh,* 1981, No. 20, p. 22.

endlessly, here or there."[12] "The Party committee of the enterprise was unable to choose the main link in its work, to concentrate efforts . . . on the most important parts. Like an implacable fireman, the Party committee threw itself from side to side. . . . "[13] "Some members of the Party apparatus drown in current affairs."[14]

To scatter one's resources is to become *ineffective*. "If at the conferences of the bureau of the Party committee, of the Party organization . . . too many questions are discussed, it is impossible to prepare them well."[15] The reconstruction of a large factory after the War proceeded "without a concentration of forces . . . without the creation, if I may say so, of a fist for striking (*udarnyi kulak*). . . . We acted, so to speak, not with a fist, but with spread fingers. But that does not make for a strong strike."[16]

To concentrate, in contrast, is to avoid being dominated by events, "to *liberate oneself* from the power of current affairs."[17] To concentrate is to dominate. "Let us underscore it again and again: the mission of the Party committee . . . consists in this: from the mass of affairs with which life threatens to overwhelm us, it is capable of separating out the . . . main ones . . . and concentrating efforts on them."[18]

To concentrate is to apply large amounts of managerial time/energy to a given issue, and thus to *enhance yield*. "We took the path of reducing the number of questions considered so as to improve the quality of preparation and of the fulfillment of decisions. We prepare every month only one . . . question for consideration in the sessions of the bureau. But we prepare it thoroughly. . . . "[19]

Concentration should be adopted *in every domain*. "The plenum must put an end to the scattering of forces and means in science. . . . "[20] "It is indispensable to obtain . . . a concentration of the efforts of scholars on the most significant problems of culture-building."[21]

---

[12]A manager, quoted by L. Brezhnev, *Tselina*, Brezhnev 1979, p. 122.

[13]V. Lozovoi, *P*, June 15, 1981.

[14]V. Shevchuk, *PZh*, 1981, No. 17, p. 43.

[15]V. Orlov, *PZh*, 1972, No. 2, p. 21.

[16]L. Brezhnev, *Vozrozhdenie*, Brezhnev 1979, p. 67.

[17]K. Chernenko 1978, p. 28. Emphasis added.

[18]K. Chernenko, *K*, 1981, No. 13, p. 13.

[19]The secretary of a Party district committee, quoted by M. Odineds, *P*, October 28, 1981.

[20]Paraphrase of L. Brezhnev's speech at the Central Committee plenum of November 1981, *P*, November 21, 1981.

[21]P. Demichev, *K*, 1981, No. 8, p. 29.

There is, by implication, likely to be *one* set of targets among the many possible ones, concentrating on which will have a much higher yield than any alternative allocation of one's resources. Thus "the ascertainment of those links by whose seizure we can pull out the whole chain remains of decisive importance for us."[22]

The *ability* to discover "main links" and then to concentrate on them is a rare skill, and one required of a leader. He must know how "to find the main link among innumerable current affairs,"[23] how "to choose among a number of important problems the most important ones. . . . "[24] "The communist leader knows how to concentrate . . . attention on the decisive sector, not scattering himself in work. . . . "[25] He possesses "the ability to concentrate on the main links, to gather forces into one fist."[26] The fist, we know, is effective, spread fingers are not. "The breakdown of the . . . assembly line conveyor began precisely in Workshop No. 3 . . . where very few communists were working, and those in second-rank positions. It was on this link . . . that the *Party* organization . . . concentrated attention. Many experienced Party members disposed to take the initiative were directed there"[27]—in contrast to "the activity of the *ministries* in charge of construction which was characterized by an inability to ascertain the main questions."[28] While success, of course, "is dependent . . . on our ability to concentrate . . . activities . . . on key directions."[29]

As there is a downward flow of *aktivnost* from the Central Committee through the several levels of the Party to the masses (see Chap. I), there is a parallel flow of the capacity to concentrate. "The Province Committee of the Party as well as the city and district committees help the Popular Controllers to concentrate forces on the main directions following from the decisions of the 26th Congress of the CPSU and of the May 1982 plenum of the Central Committee of the Party. Only on this condition will the People's Control be ever more . . . effective. . . . "[30]

---

[22]L. Brezhnev, *Vozrozhdenie*, Brezhnev 1979, p. 68.

[23]G. Kalugin, *PZh*, 1972, No. 14, p. 46.

[24]A. Pelshe, *K*, 1981, No. 11, p. 8.

[25]Editorial, *PZh*, 1979, No. 14, p. 7.

[26]V. Shangin, *PZh*, 1981, No. 3, p. 62.

[27]V. Vorotnikov, *P*, October 8, 1981. Emphasis added.

[28]Unsigned article, *PZh*, 1978, No. 1, p. 29. Emphasis added.

[29]Yu. Andropov, Central Committee plenum, November 22, 1982, FBIS, November 23, p. R-9. Emphasis added.

[30]V. Klyuev, First Secretary of the Ivanov Province Committee of the Party, *P*, October 12, 1982.

Chapter IV

INTERMITTENCE (*PRERYVISTOST'*)

Ordinary human beings, it has come to the notice of the Party leadership, are inclined—yielding to their penchant for inaction (Chap. I)—not only to stop prematurely an action in which they are engaged (Chap. II), but also to act with intermissions more frequent and extensive than are optimal. This penchant is likely to render the entire operation ineffective. "There occur, of course, critical pronouncements in the press and on television, and sometimes in films and plays, hitting these defects. But an *uninterrupted*, massed attack is . . . not conducted."[1]

Whenever subordinates stop acting, superiors seem to be seized by anguish. Will they ever start up anew? Or will they not rather stop for good at what they have already achieved and thus lose even that? "The main point in the decisions of the Central Committee plenum of May 1972 is the requirement that every communist . . . not even *for one instant* cease to feel the Leninist Party spirit."[2] Will they ever return to what they have been capable of abandoning? Or, if they do return this time, will they the next?

Hence, "in this important direction"—and which direction is unimportant?—"one must work unwearyingly."[3] Of any task it may be said: "This task . . . requires . . . uninterrupted effort."[4] This requirement is often expressed in terms of the inclination thus rejected. "The choice and deployment of cadres is not . . . an act of a moment but . . . an interrupted process."[5] Of any direction of activity it may be said that it entails "not a campaign of short duration, but daily action of Party . . . organizations."[6] "This is not a campaign. . . . this is our systematic work,"[7] conducted not "from case to case" but "consistently," that is, uninterruptedly. "Demands [of performance] are to be raised not from case to case, but continuously, daily."[8] "Party organizations are required to conduct not episodic but continuous

[1]Unsigned article, *K*, 1982, No. 1, p. 32. Emphasis added.

[2]Unsigned article, *PZh*, 1972, No. 16, p. 42. Emphasis added.

[3]M. Suslov, speech, October 16, 1979, *K*, 1979, No. 15, p. 37.

[4]K. Chernenko, *K*, 1982, No. 6, p. 25.

[5]I. Polyakov, *PZh*, 1973, No. 4, p. 9.

[6]Editorial, *K*, 1971, No. 14, p. 7.

[7]V. Shcherbitskii, *PZh*, 1981, No. 15, p. 39.

[8]V. Shangin, *PZh*, 1980, No. 7, p. 50.

. . . work. . . . "[9] "*Kontrol'* is effective . . . if it is realized not in an episodic manner but continuously. . . . "[10] "The accent was laid on the creation of a permanent system of measures, for there is no lack of episodic verification."[11]

A requirement for "uninterruptedness" may be stressed with regard to an activity that to a Westerner seems to need that quality so clearly as to render a demand for it superfluous. "The struggle for economy and preservation (*berezhlivost'*) transformed itself into an uninterrupted process. . . . "[12] "The fight against instability of personnel is an uninterrupted process, requiring daily attention. . . . "[13] "Management is an uninterrupted chain of decisions."[14]

Similarly, the *presence* of uninterruptedness may be stressed with regard to events where it might be taken for granted by a Westerner. "Social life does not come to a halt even for an instant."[15]

On the other hand, uninterruptedness on pain of failure may be required in situations where it might seem dispensable to a Westerner. "The effectiveness of criticism and self-criticism is obtained in the same conditions in which *kontrol'* is effective, that is, when one has recourse to it constantly . . . and not intermittently, from case to case."[16]

Just as, in the Party leadership's combat against inaction, only strenuous work is credited with effectiveness, so here with regard to intermittence in acting. Anything that is pursued "seriously"—and what should not be?—has to be done uninterruptedly. "Heightening the role of the province and district committees of the Party is a . . . serious and . . . continuous task."[17] One ought to introduce and maintain "systems securing the uninterruptedness of . . . education,"[18] for the effectiveness of ideological-political work depends to a large extent on its uninterruptedness. . . . "[19]

Any development that is good is also uninterrupted. Thus Marxism-Leninism is an "uninterruptedly developing doctrine,"[20]

---

[9]Editorial, *K*, 1971, No. 14, p. 13.

[10]N. Shvats, *PZh*, 1980, No. 9, p. 39.

[11]G. Bartshevich, *P*, July 27, 1980.

[12]V. Brovikov, *K*, 1972, No. 7, p. 80.

[13]V. Solopov, *PZh*, 1980, No. 17, p. 45.

[14]V. Shcherbitskii 1978, p. 205.

[15]A. Pelshe, quoted in an editorial, *PZh*, 1979, No. 13, p. 12.

[16]I. Gustov, *PZh*, 1980, No. 19, p. 21.

[17]Editorial, *PZh*, 1981, No. 8, p. 40.

[18]V. Makeev, *PZh*, 1979, No. 14, p. 30.

[19]V. Grishin, speech, September 14, 1977, Grishin 1979, p. 421.

[20]Resolution of the Central Committee at the occasion of the 110th birthday of Lenin, quoted in M. Suslov, *K*, 1980, No. 4, p. 16.

"Leninism . . . is the uninterrupted self-renewal of revolutionary theory,"[21] and "the Leninist style of work . . . developed uninterruptedly. . . . "[22]

Perceiving, I surmise, an uninterrupted downward pressure of spontaneity, the Party leadership counters with the requirement of an equally uninterrupted upward movement. "It is necessary to heighten uninterruptedly the level of work . . . "[23] on anything, "uninterruptedly to increase the effectiveness of Party organizations,"[24] to obtain "the uninterrupted heightening of the level of the Party leadership in economy and culture."[25]

Of course, one must strive uninterruptedly for such uninterrupted improvement, must engage in "unswerving striving for an uninterrupted perfecting [of one's style of work]," for "the uninterrupted improvement . . . of all forms of work. . . . "[26] Then, perhaps only then, can one be sure that one is not falling, and so ceasing to be.

---

[21]Yu. Andropov, quoted in *K*, 1980, No. 5, p. 120.

[22]Unsigned article, *PZh*, 1978, No. 4, p. 34.

[23]*PZh*, 1978, No. 4, p. 26.

[24]K. Chernenko 1978, p. 62.

[25]Unsigned article, *PZh*, 1978, No. 20, p. 15.

[26]K. Chernenko 1980, p. 394.

Chapter V

WASTING TIME

When acting spontaneously, the Party's leadership seems to believe, human beings are insufficiently aware of time. Yet he "who is not accustomed to account for every working minute will never attain high results."[1] It becomes appropriate then to demand that "in the work on perfecting the direction of the economy, full account be taken of the factor of time. In the domain of planning this means keeping a precise account not only of monetary means and resources, but also of the time that the realization of various projects requires."[2]

The penchant for inaction idles people during a good part of the time designated for working, "With us [a factory] there are . . . losses of working time the liquidation of which requires neither material expenditures nor supplementary mechanization or automatization . . . but only one thing . . . an honest fulfillment of the obligation with which one is charged."[3] "In factories and building sites, in kolkhozes and sovkhozes, much time is still wasted. . . . "[4] "On many construction sites the workers do not have to work so much as [merely] to stand there."[5] "It often happens. People come to work on time, but then do not find work for hours or even days."[6]

Hence "the slogan 'For every minute of the Five-Year Plan—an account of work done!'"[7] "Conserve working time!"[8] "Utilize every working hour with maximum effectiveness!"[9] "The main thing . . . is to arrange matters so that a worker is occupied with work in the course of the working day from the first to the last minute."[10]

Not losing working time is praiseworthy. "Not one minute of working time is lost by this advanced worker. As a result, his output is double that that others realize with similar equipment."[11]

---

[1]Editorial, *P*, October 13, 1982.

[2]L. Brezhnev, 25th Party Congress, February 24, 1976, Brezhnev 1976, p. 518.

[3]A. Kornienko, *PZh*, 1979, No. 1, p. 51.

[4]Unsigned article, *PZh*, 1981, No. 9, p. 67.

[5]Editorial, *P*, February 4, 1983.

[6]Editorial, *PZh*, 1983, No. 7, p. 5.

[7]A. Kornienko, *PZh*, 1979, No. 1, p. 47.

[8]Headline, *P*, September 22, 1980.

[9]Slogan reported in an editorial, *P*, September 22, 1980.

[10]A factory manager, interviewed by A. Chernyak, *P*, November 29, 1982.

[11]Editorial, *P*, April 8, 1980.

* * * * * * * *

The urge to inaction may make one slow in starting to act, may delay acting. There is "a tendency to delay tackling a difficult problem."[12] "It is no secret," runs a major theme, "that in a series of enterprises new technique is often adopted slowly. . . . "[13] "The new economic mechanism replaces the old one only slowly . . . there remains the most important thing, not to drag its introduction out over years."[14] "Many undertakings are discussed at length, repeatedly approved, but only slowly and unwillingly acted upon."[15]

Being late may be viewed as normal. "If a person passes through the entrance of the factory before the minute of the beginning of the shift, this is not counted as being late. But . . . he is going to begin working at the earliest after 10 to 15 minutes."[16]

Not being late is worth praise. "Are there not many agreements [in "socialist competition"] which . . . consist in obligations of the type 'appearing for work without being late?'"[17] "In the brigade that he [a model worker] heads, not one 'petty detail' is neglected. For instance, if somebody is late at work, this is an extraordinary event. In other brigades nobody pays attention to such an event: this (the saying goes) . . . happens to everybody."[18] "Precisely at the announced hour the Secretary of the Party Committee of the kolkhoz 'Ukraina' . . . opened the meeting. All communists who were able to be present were already there. Not one was late."[19] Such conformity to the norm is, of course, produced by high effort: "At the first interruption of the meeting I told the Secretary: 'You must have worked a good bit so as to obtain such presence and precision in the beginning of the meeting.'"[20] Under the headline, "A Person Who Takes His Duty Seriously," the first point made is: "He is not late for work, he meets a friend in time . . . he comes to the meeting at the appointed hour."[21]

The disposition to delay is much opposed. *Neotlozhno*, literally "what should not be deferred," is a key word for "urgent." "The matter

---

[12]Editorial, *P*, April 4, 1983.

[13]*PZh*, 1977, No. 6, p. 32.

[14]V. Parfenov, *P*, August 10, 1981.

[15]Editorial, *PZh*, 1979, No. 14, p. 7.

[16]A worker, quoted in F. Loshchenko, *K*, 1970, No. 1, p. 27.

[17]Editorial, *K*, 1971, No. 14, p. 9.

[18]G. Boskanyan, *P*, July 10, 1982.

[19]V. Tolstov, *PZh*, 1970, No. 21, p. 58.

[20]Ibid.

[21]Editorial, *P*, April 4, 1982.

brooks no delay" is a set phrase.[22] "One should not, as the phrase goes, sit by the sea and wait for good weather,"[23] should not engage in "passive waiting."[24] One should "discuss the question and decide it right away, not deferring," so that "the question can be decided without delay."[25] "In order to realize [something] in full measure . . . it is necessary already today, without losing time, to. . . . "[26] "The communists expressed this opinion: already today it is necessary to make a major contribution to the realization of the plans of the Party. Already today . . . [emphasis in the original—NL]."[27] Indeed, the rejection of delay furnishes the occasion for a rare acknowledgment of tradeoffs: "It is often expedient to renounce . . . fullness of information . . . but by that to . . . make a decision in good time."[28]

There is a disposition to replace steady ("rhythmical") work toward a completion date by a deadline schedule initially calling for low exertion followed by a terminal crash effort, or "storming" (*shturm, avral'*), usually of a defective kind (Chap. VII). One may note "the practice of planning to turn out only 30 to 40 percent of the yearly production program during the first half year."[29] "In many construction collectives there is at present [early in the year] a lull. . . . Before us, they say, there is time; it will be possible to catch up on what has not been done."[30] "Yearly tasks in construction are planned so that the completion of the majority of objects is foreseen for the fourth quarter. This leads to storming (*shturmovshchina*). . . . "[31] Many "managers really fight for plans only during the last ten days of the month.[32] "Up to 70 percent of production [of certain goods] are habitually produced during the last ten days of the month. How then could there not be defects in products?"[33] "It is well known that the largest fraction of faulty products comes from the last hours of the month when 'they storm the plan.'"[34]

---

[22]V. Legostaev, *PZh*, 1980, No. 5, p. 40.

[23]V. Murakhovskii, quoted by A. Chernyak, *P*, December 1, 1981.

[24]M. Mikhailov, *K*, 1981, No. 8, p. 115.

[25]A. Mendeleev, *PZh*, 1981, No. 2, p. 45.

[26]Editorial, *P*, July 15, 1982.

[27]Editorial, *P*, November 19, 1982.

[28]K. Chernenko 1980, pp. 181–182.

[29]*K*, 1975, No. 16, p. 11.

[30]Editorial, *P*, February 15, 1980.

[31]Editorial, *P*, October 9, 1980.

[32]I. Bondarenko, *PZh*, 1974, No. 19, p. 23.

[33]N. Aralin and N. Motsalin, *P*, April 10, 1980.

[34]Editorial, *K*, 1976, No. 11, p. 6.

"It is time," the Party leadership keeps objecting, "to firmly understand this truth: uneven production can never be effective."[35] "Making up for what has been omitted—we must remember this—is always harder and not always successful."[36] "From the very outset of the Five-Year Plan one must work with a full giving of one's forces and a full yield."[37]

* * * * * * * *

If one is slow in starting, one may also be slow in acting. Dragging out an operation appears to the leadership to be a more important vice than "precipitation." About any operation it may be said that "one ought to work at higher speed."[38] It is appropriate to warn that "new questions arise which must be solved without delay."[39] In an area favored in climate, road network, and labor, "it is hard to find a big construction area in which the timing of efforts was maintained 'from the pit to the key.'"[40] Although "it is impossible to justify protracted construction . . . in certain regions and economic departments the reaction to it is highly benign."[41] Again and again "something that should have taken five minutes was dragged out over two hours."[42] Similarly, "the time taken to complete some most important construction is being dragged out."[43] In fact, "there are many important economic projects whose construction and reconstruction are protracted for ten to fifteen years, or even longer. Thus the expansion of the Novosibirsk factory of electroaggregates has dragged on for 18 years, while only 60 percent of the allotted funds have been spent; and the entry of the enterprise into production is not foreseen for the present Five-Year Plan. The new capacities in the factory 'Tomkabel' have been in construction for eight years instead of the two years foreseen. Only a third of the work has been accomplished, and the end is not in view. The term for the accomplishment of the work has been changed six times. . . . "[44]

---

[35]A. Kirilenko, *PZh*, 1978, No. 6, p. 12.

[36]G. Romanov, speech, January 14, 1982, *Leningradskaya Pravda*, January 15, FBIS, January 28, p. R-13.

[37]L. Brezhnev, at a Central Committee plenum, October 25, 1976, Brezhnev 1978, p. 148.

[38]Editorial, *P*, September 29, 1982.

[39]L. Brezhnev, speech, October 27, 1982, *P*, October 28, 1982.

[40]Ya. Mogoryan, *P*, September 23, 1981.

[41]Editorial, *K*, 1978, No. 18, p. 11.

[42]L. Brezhnev, *Vozrozhdenie*, Brezhnev 1979, p. 67.

[43]Editorial, *P*, June 14, 1980.

[44]Editorial, *K*, 1979, No. 8, p. 8.

One factor making for such a result is the dispersion of resources (see Chap. III). "The residual estimated cost of objects begun by the Ministry of Industrial Construction of the USSR exceeds 30 billion rubles. To complete them even without beginning new ones . . . more than five years will be required, while according to norms, the duration of the majority of the projects should not go beyond two to three years."[45] "In Penza Province at the Bashnakovo Station a silo has been in construction for several years. It was supposed to have begun functioning last year. . . . Why [this delay]? The builders did not concentrate forces and means on this object. . . . "[46]

But there is also the complicity of the Party: "If the Party organizations of Chelyabinsk Province had concerned themselves more energetically with the . . . entry into operation of new factories, we would have had last year a supplementary output of more than 200,000 tons of cast iron, and of more than half a million tons of steel. . . . "[47] "The reconstruction of the [railway] was dragged out. The first stage of this work was finished in 1978. . . . To hasten its completion, the help of the Yaroslav division of the railway was needed. However, the Party Bureau and the direction of the station assumed a waiting position. They did not pointedly put before the higher-level body the question of hastening the completion of that industrial object. . . . "[48]

The date beyond which an operation may be "dragged out" is one on which users counted. "A serious obstacle in the work of a number of collectives remains the violation of discipline in delivery"—[49] owing in part to the introduction and maintenance of perverse incentives (which, I conjecture, themselves express in part the inclination toward slowness). "The managers of enterprises . . . receive premiums even when they fulfill orders only to the extent of 90 to 95 percent."[50] In addition, "the penalities imposed on those who violate economic agreements are insufficient. For instance, the Dnepropetrovsk Supply Office in the past years exacted from the metallurgical factories of the district less than the tenth part of the penalties imposed."[51]

In such conditions "disruptions in deliveries destroy the rhythm of production and in the end inflict damage on the economy."[52] Party

---

[45]A. Chekalin, *P*, February 8, 1982.

[46]Editorial, *K*, No. 1, p. 7.

[47]D. Ustinov, speech, February 21, 1968, Ustinov 1979, p. 138.

[48]A. Urov, *PZh*, 1980, No. 3, p. 52.

[49]Editorial, *P*, January 3, 1981.

[50]Editorial, *P*, May 12, 1980.

[51]Ibid.

[52]Editorial, *P*, September 29, 1982.

leadership advances the slogan, "All deliveries on schedule!"[53] "Dozens of collectives have joined the movement with the motto, 'All deliveries on schedule!' Hundreds of factories and construction enterprises have become involved in the work relay (*rabochaya estafeta*). On the other hand, it cannot be considered normal that favorable places in socialist competition are more than once awarded to enterprises . . . that violate the dates of deliveries to customers. It is important to fulfill all orders of customers precisely on the planned dates!"[54]

Yet after decades of such counteraction, one may observe that "in a series of branches of production and of regions, the slogan 'all orders on time' has in fact been forgotten."[55]

Being on time in this perspective is a mark of excellence. "During the last years the managers of the Kuznets Metallurgical *Kombinat* . . . were blamelessly precise in all deliveries."[56] "Orders are fulfilled punctually by the Moscow machinebuilding factory in the name of Serge Ordzhonikidze, the Novopolotsk association 'Polimir,' the Tashkent tractor factory, the Vilna factory for heating equipment, 'Dneproshina,' and others."[57]

Being "ahead of time" (another major theme) is even better: surely one is then not late. "Let us build ahead of time and implement in good time (*dosrochno postroim-posrochno usvoim*)!"[58] "Many advanced workers have already reported on the accomplishment of their personal five-year and yearly tasks ahead of schedule. Among those who are ahead of schedule are. . . . "[59] Thus it is shown that "we communists are capable of solving the biggest tasks within a short time"[60]—at rates that are not only high but increasing, and thus hold the assurance that one is *not* losing speed, not headed for a standstill, which is death.

---

[53]Headline, *P*, June 15, 1981.

[54]Ibid.

[55]Editorial, *K*, 1982, No. 3, p. 9.

[56]Editorial, *K*, 1975, No. 16, p. 5.

[57]Editorial, *P*, February 12, 1983.

[58]Headline of editorial, *P*, February 15, 1980.

[59]Editorial, *P*, December 11, 1980.

[60]L. Brezhnev, *Tselina*, Brezhnev 1979, p. 140.

Chapter VI

FAILURE TO CALCULATE (*NEPRODUMANNOST'*)

Human beings are, in the belief of the Party leadership, given to uncalculated and then surely harmful action, to "hotheadedness," to "hastiness of conclusions and conduct."[1] "There is much fuss, strain on nerves, and often pointless, empty activity."[2] "We acted," one may disclose about a part of one's own past which is remote and in which one had no determining part, "on the principle that 'something may turn up,'"[3] or "on the off chance." It is appropriate to point out about any undertaking that "*neprodumannost*" can only be harmful here.[4]

Hence the requirement "not to be hasty in arriving at conclusions, to think a good deal."[5] "Hence, the slogan advanced by Comrade L. I. Brezhnev at the November 1971 plenum of the Central Committee of the CPSU: 'Think and learn.'"[6] "It must become a law for each economic manager not to begin the construction of new objects without a project and estimate."[7]

"Communists," it may be alleged, in contrast to ordinary humans, "take upon themselves . . . obligations that have been thought through deeply";[8] that are, in a well-known point, derived from "science." "The activity of the Central Committee of the CPSU is characterized by a scientific approach"—[9] which may coincide with common sense, as when "it is inadmissible to appoint just anybody to executive positions. . . . [Such appointments should rather be] well considered, expressing a scientific approach to the selection and promotion of cadres."[10]

It seems appropriate to insist that having an adequate rationale for one's conduct enhances the chances of success. "The Party organizations of the kolkhoz and sovkhoz in Kiev Province had to undergo a difficult examination [by weather] this year. They passed with honor

---

[1]A. Litovchenko, *P*, July 27, 1981.

[2]N. Khamov, *P*, January 27, 1980.

[3]L. Brezhnev, *Tselina*, Brezhnev 1979, p. 122.

[4]V. Rostovshchikov, *P*, April 24, 1982.

[5]P. Loshchenko, *K*, 1970, No. 1, p. 25.

[6]G. Romanov, *K*, 1972, No. 5, p. 52.

[7]L. Brezhnev, speech, at the 24th Party Congress, March 30, 1971, Brezhnev 1972, p. 264.

[8]F. Kozyrev, *PZh*, 1972, No. 3, p. 48.

[9]V. Shcherbitskii, *K*, 1980, No. 6, p. 19.

[10]A. Pelshe, *K*, 1980, No. 2, p. 24.

mainly because they acted in a thought-out manner, precisely taking account of concrete conditions."[11]

People are inclined to forget that what they are doing should be a means to an end. "Some managers act thoughtlessly with regard to the modernization of production, investing large means in it. But they forget to aim at final results."[12]

What then becomes a requirement is the acquisition and exercise of "the ability to approach the solution of any task from the point of view of final results,"[13] "the capacity to put a clear goal before oneself,"[14] that is, to view anything else as an instrument for its attainment. "In no case should [a] search become an end in itself."[15] Thus, "there should be a closer connection between the plans for construction and the tasks of the collectives that are to use the construction. Construction for which there is no confirmed documentation [as to future use] should not be included in plans. . . . One should work with the motto, 'For every new construction there should be an . . . economic project.'"[16]

Calculation, or purposefulness (*tseleustremlennost', tselenapravlennost'*), is needed for excellence. "Any *serious* operation is preceded by a calculation. First, one must determine for what purpose . . . and how one must act, and only afterward may one begin execution." This is how certain collectives actually behave. "Thus believe the cadres of the Department of Light and Food Industry of the Communist Party of Lithuania. Thus they try hard to act."[17]

"It must be underscored that, as was observed at the Party Congress, the work of the plenums [of the Central Committee], of the Politburo, and of the Secretariat of the Central Committee of the CPSU bore a purposeful character. . . . "[18]

* * * * * * * *

One component of "purposefulness" is "definiteness."

Spontaneity is apt to produce decisions that are "diffuse."[19] "Often decisions bear a *general* character . . . *do not foresee any real mea-*

---

[11]V. Tsybulko, *PZh*, 1972, No. 24, p. 31.

[12]I. Klimenko, *P*, April 29, 1981.

[13]L. Brezhnev, *Vozrozhdenie*, Brezhnev 1979, p. 68.

[14]A. Urov, *PZh*, 1980, No. 3, p. 48.

[15]K. Chernenko 1980, p. 205.

[16]Editorial, *P*, June 9, 1981.

[17]M. Poltoranin and D. Shnyukas, *P*, July 19, 1981.

[18]Unsigned article, *PZh*, 1981, No. 8, p. 61.

[19]V. Grishin, *PZh*, 1972, No. 1, p. 16.

sures."[20] "The following . . . occurs: a Party meeting . . . notes a certain defect and adopts a decision to remove it. However, the decision proposes *no concrete* measures."[21] "In May of last year the plenum of the District considered the tasks of the District Party organization [with regard] to heightening the effectiveness of. . . . All 13 points of the decision taken were couched in general expressions such as 'to strengthen,' 'to secure,' 'to activate.'"[22]

> When there is *no* . . . *specific* analysis, then nothing remains in the section [of a resolution] dealing with . . . solutions except for the words "oblige," "eliminate," "reinforce," "enhance." Once, in preparing for a meeting of the Republic [Estonia] Communist Party Central Committee *apparat,* I pasted over the headline and name of the organization on a text of resolution, and then, having read it out, suggested to my comrades that they name the document and the institution to which it related. . . . Not one responded, although there were persons present who had taken part in composing the document quoted.[23]

Lack of definiteness in a decision reduces the performance oriented on it. In the reconstruction of a factory after the War, "people were working without norms. . . . They based their work on what can be achieved . . . and not on what it is necessary to do."[24] "What the District Committee intended to realize was not done, mainly because not all of its decisions were distinguished by concreteness. . . . "[25]

Also, because lack of concreteness in a decision is an obstacle to *kontrol'* (see Chap. I) over it. "Sometimes the decisions taken were so general and empty that it was . . . impossible to exercise *kontrol'* over their fulfillment."[26] "The resolution adopted by the meeting consisted of general expressions—to heighten, to improve, to continue. It will be extremely difficult for the Party organization to verify its fulfillment."[27] "If there is no precise plan . . . we have no means in our hands with which to exercise *kontrol'*, to demand, to encourage, and if

---

[20]N. Shvats, *PZh*, 1980, No. 9, p. 42. Emphasis added.

[21]V. Smirnov, *PZh*, 1973, No. 4, p. 44. Emphasis added.

[22]V. Tsurilov, *PZh*, 1980, No. 24, p. 59.

[23]K. Vaino, First Secretary of the Estonian Central Committee, *P*, June 7, 1981. Emphasis added.

[24]L. Brezhnev, *Vozrozhdenie*, Brezhnev 1979, p. 64.

[25]V. Tsurilov, *PZh*, 1980, No. 24, p. 59.

[26]A. Urov, *PZh*, 1980, No. 3, p. 52.

[27]V. Legostaev, *PZh*, 1980, No. 17, p. 50.

need be, to punish"—and "then there will be sharp movement forward."[28]

On the other hand, "a precise plan accelerates performance."[29]

Hence the requirement of "precise directedness,"[30] of "thinking the matter through *in detail.*"[31] "Every worker must . . . give not general recommendations but. . . . "[32] "There should always be a precise plan of action."[33] "Every work collective, every worker must . . . precisely know the goal that he must reach. . . . "[34] "All our decisions must be reinforced by . . . organizational measures. [It should be indicated] what must be done where and within what time span, who is responsible for a given sector of work, who verifies fulfillment."[35]

Definiteness—"leaving no place for indeterminateness"[36]—is a mark of excellence. "Before the communists [of a factory] were put precise objectives, definite paths toward their attainment."[37] "The instructions of the Party Committee are distinguished by . . . the concreteness of the tasks set and always having a precise address."[38]

"It is a task of the Party organization to form in every communist a position in life that is . . . precisely determinate"[39] —that is, indeterminate on *no* issue. "At the voting in Party organizations the chairman asks: who is 'for,' who is 'against,' who 'abstains?'" Yet "is it permissible for a communist to abstain? I believe not. To abstain is to doubt something. But a Party member must always have a *clear* and *hard* conception about everything."[40]

* * * * * * * *

A decision may be precise and internally correct, yet may neglect to specify whether the resources required for its realization are available—that is, may fail to determine "to what extent the decision is

---

[28]L. Brezhnev, *Vozrozhdenie*, Brezhnev 1979, p. 65.

[29]Headline, *P*, April 17, 1980.

[30]V. Shcherbitskii, 1978, p. 142.

[31]Headline, *P*, September 15, 1980. Emphasis added.

[32]G. Bandrovskii, *PZh*, 1980, No. 17, p. 44.

[33]A. Rybakov, *K*, 1974, No. 10, p. 52.

[34]L. Brezhnev, at a Central Committee plenum, October 25, 1976, Brezhnev 1978, p. 173.

[35]L. Brezhnev, at the November 1978 plenum of the Central Committee, quoted in an unsigned article, *PZh*, 1979, No. 10, p. 54.

[36]K. Chernenko 1980, p. 357.

[37]V. Liventsov, *P*, June 17, 1980.

[38]G. Belov, *PZh*, 1980, No. 6, p. 48.

[39]A. Pelshe, *K*, 1980, No. 2, p. 32.

[40]V. Ushakov, *PZh*, 1978, No. 7, p. 71. Emphasis added.

well grounded rather than "bare scheming."[41] "It happens that plans are established . . . without a serious analysis . . . of real possibilities."[42] "Obligations [in socialist competition] are adopted without taking account of possibilities."[43] "Are decisions taken always . . . connected with financial and material resources? Far from always."[44] "Decisions" may be wishful thinking (*plany-pozhelaniya*), "not supported by corresponding material-technical resources"—instances of "the still continuing practice of distributing 'air' (*raspredelenie vozdukha*),"[45] of taking "decisions that are not given strength by real material bases."[46] "Sometimes tasks fully set, particularly as to the year in which construction projects are to be delivered, are not balanced with the possibilities of work collectives and their material-technical resources."[47] "In [some] plans the dimensions of construction as well as the number of objects to be built are increased without taking account of real possibilities."[48] "In the report to the Central Committee plenum of Georgia in June of this year it was observed that, for the fulfillment of the decisions on construction taken by the Central Committee and the Council of Ministers of the Republic, more than 800,000,000 rubles were lacking which were practically unavailable."[49] "Sometimes precise . . . resolutions are not fulfilled. For even disciplined subordinates may be put into conditions where they cannot keep their word. This occurs when . . . tasks beyond their forces are put before them. For instance, the factory in the name of N. V. Frunze, building agricultural machines, was . . . planned to produce this year 5000 [units of a certain kind]. But the factory in Kursk furnishing . . . components for these [units] was ready to deliver enough only for 3500."[50] "What can even the best collective do if the plan requires amounts that cannot be obtained . . . with the available equipment, raw materials, and labor force. . . ?"[51] Thus "often . . . the failure in the work of this or that collective [the nonfulfillment of its plan] is inherent in the task itself as

---

[41] *PZh*, 1978, No. 2, p. 32.

[42] K. Chernenko 1980, p. 185.

[43] Editorial, *P*, January 11, 1982.

[44] L. Brezhnev, at the November 1978 Central Committee plenum, quoted by N. Shvats, *PZh*, 1980, No. 9, p. 42.

[45] B. Odlis, *K*, 1980, No. 1, p. 81.

[46] K. Chernenko 1978, p. 13.

[47] Editorial, *P*, July 23, 1980.

[48] L. Brezhnev, speech at the 24th Party Congress, March 30, 1971, Brezhnev 1972, p. 264.

[49] K. Bogolyubov, PZh, 1981, No. 20, p. 26.

[50] K. Fomichenko, *P*, July 20, 1980.

[51] Editorial, *K*, 1980, No. 9, p. 9.

determined by the planning organs; the plan was badly furnished with materials and other resources."[52]

It may be deemed worthwhile to doubt the power of intentions: "A mere wish to fully renovate industry is still insufficient. What is needed is the means, so as to order technological lines and put them into operation."[53] "Life has shown it is impossible to embrace the unembraceable."[54]

It is also appropriate to insist on the *benefits* of paying attention to what is feasible. "*It is known* that successes in construction-. . . depend on the measure in which plans correspond to material-technical resources."[55] "*Experience shows* that the solution of a question depends on . . . the realism of the intended operation. It is well known that there is little point to documents . . . that do not take account of the situation and are weakly supported in material, organizational, and ideological respects."[56] "To weigh one's forces before saying one's word is a necessary condition for its fulfillment. But not all bother to do that."[57]

One may enunciate a *requirement* to take account of what is feasible. "The decision of the Central Committee of the CPSU and of the Council of Ministers of the USSR . . . notes the necessity of tying building plans more fully with material-technical resources. . . . "[58] "One should weigh at every step whether material and other resources are available for the realization of a plan, and whether the time spans indicated are sufficient."[59] "One must build as one lives, within one's means."[60]

In its early years the Brezhnev regime set itself off from its predecessor as more obedient to this principle: "The new approach to the solution of economic problems that . . . was manifested in the activity of Party organizations after the Central Committee plenum of October 1964 . . . became more thought-through and . . . well grounded,"[61] more sober. What is required, it was declared in the late Brezhnev era, is "sobriety in evaluating the situation; not simply precision, but precisely

---

[52]Editorial, *P*, October 15, 1981.

[53]M. Poltoranin and D. Shnyukas, *P*, July 20, 1981.

[54]V. Goncharov, *P*, May 31, 1981.

[55]Editorial, *P*, October 9, 1980. Emphasis added.

[56]N. Umanets, *P*, July 3, 1981. Emphasis added.

[57]A. Kolesnikov, *P*, August 29, 1980.

[58]Editorial, *P*, October 9, 1980.

[59]A. Kirilenko, *PZh*, 1978, No. 6, p. 20.

[60]L. Brezhnev, speech at the 24th Party Congress, March 30, 1971, Brezhnev 1972, p. 264.

[61]Editorial, *K*, 1971, No. 4, p. 7.

sobriety. The obstacles before us are real. Not to take account of them is to make a mistake."[62]

Yet what is thus rejected returns in the guise of the assertion that feasibilities are always likely to be larger than they seem; that there are in every situation "deep reserves of production"[63] that only the Party is able to discover and utilize. "A valuable initiative always uncovers a fresh layer of new possibilities which have up to now not been utilized."[64]

Lacking "sobriety," one will underestimate the amount of resources and time required to attain an objective (see Chap. II), particularly under stress: "A competent manager is accounting for his work to the bureau of the Party Province Committee. Things in the enterprise headed by him are not going so well. He admits that. And then he boldly asserts that he will remedy the situation within days. This despite the fact that it is perfectly well known that months of stubborn work will be required."[65] Hence the pertinence of insisting, "You are not going to do this at once, with a single stroke."[66] "This objective cannot be seized at one dash, by storming, with one swoop."[67] "It would be a serious mistake to turn this work into a short-term campaign."[68] "Naturally, you cannot automatize production with a single stroke."[69] "On some matters the Party Group acted right away, and on others it worked for a considerable time; you cannot always conquer in one swoop."[70] About anything it may be stressed that it is a "difficult and protracted process"[71]—all the more reason not to drag it out (Chap. V).

* * * * * * * *

Spontaneity, as the preceding pages of this chapter imply, does not favor preparation. "Why be silent about sins? The ministries are in the habit of drawing [local] cadres from the spontaneous flow, not burdening themselves with their preparation."[72]

Yet lack of preparation causes failure. "At the beginning of the year, in the session of the Party bureau of the factory Avtoremles in

---

[62]E. Muraviev, *P*, April 15, 1981.

[63]Editorial, *P*, October 9, 1980.

[64]N. Kirichenko, *P*, May 26, 1980.

[65]A. Kolesnikov, *P*, August 29, 1980.

[66]A. Nanagev, *P*, June 11, 1980.

[67]A. Brygin, *K*, 1982, No. 15, p. 63.

[68]V. Golikov, *K*, 1982, No. 13.

[69]M. Poltoranin and D. Shnyukas, *P*, July 20, 1981.

[70]O. Vavilkin, *P*, July 21, 1980.

[71]Editorial, *P*, August 9, 1981.

[72]G. Pavlov, *P*, September 5, 1980.

Khabarovsk, the assistant director, V. Manyuk, and the chief of production, Yu. Polyakov, reported on their activities. No useful discussion resulted because these reports were not prepared beforehand. . . ."[73] "There are still many resolutions which have been prepared in haste. . . ."[74]

Hence, it becomes appropriate to insist on preparation, to proceed "according to a system thought out beforehand."[75] "This," the Party leadership is likely to assert about anything, "is a complicated matter. Here haste is inadmissible. A thorough and all-sided preparation is required."[76]

[73]Editorial, *P*, July 31, 1980.

[74]K. Chernenko 1980, p. 172.

[75]M. Romenenko, *P*, February 6, 1983.

[76]V. Grishin, speech, March 28, 1968, Grishin 1979, p. 104.

Chapter VII

UNEVENNESS (*NEROVNOST'*)

The Party leadership observes a penchant toward a "thoughtless shifting around of managers and specialists,"[1] and even "frequent [and] abrupt transfer of construction workers from one site to another."[2] "When the brigade is being suddenly thrown from one site to another, as if it were a fire brigade. . . . "[3] "Abrupt transfers of brigades from one construction to another have a very disturbing effect."[4] About instances of "uninterruptedly throwing an official from one post to another," such practices "took place in our city. In the metallurgical factory in the name of Ilyich there were during the last decade three directors and five secretaries of the Party Committee."[5]

Such practices were affirmed by the Brezhnev regime to have been in vogue under its predecessor, and then discontinued. "In the recent past reorganizations of Party, Soviet, and economic organs were undertaken which called forth frequent changes in the positions of cadres. . . . The removal of these defects after the October 1964 plenum of the Central Committee created normal conditions. . . . "[6] "An end has been made," Brezhnev announced at the 25th Party Congress in 1976, "to unjustified transfers of cadres, which were . . . discussed at the 23d Congress [1966]."[7] Yet in the 1980s one may apply to the present time "the expression of Comrade L. I. Brezhnev, 'the *quadrille* of the cadres,' that is, shifting people from place to place,"[8] "the juggling with cadres,"[9] "the reshuffling of cadres, which inflicts serious harm."[10] Also, "the not always necessary transfers of [construction] brigades from place to place continue."[11] "Comrade Surovtsev has manifestly become involved in all sorts of reorganizations . . . and in carrying out frequent, insufficiently justified shifts and

---

[1]Editorial, *PZh,* 1970, No. 19, p. 5.

[2]Editorial, *PZh,* 1980, No. 3, p. 26.

[3]N. Zlobin, *PZh,* 1980, No. 5, p. 20.

[4]A. Krenev, quoted in editorial, *P,* March 25, 1983.

[5]V. Zharkov, *PZh,* 1976, No. 9, p. 38.

[6]M. Mazarov, *K,* 1970, No. 1, p. 70.

[7]L. Brezhnev 1976, p. 529.

[8]I. Kapitonov, *PZh,* 1980, No. 14, p. 19.

[9]S. Manyakin, *P,* July 25, 1981.

[10]Editorial, *P,* November 13, 1981.

[11]V. Shirokov, *P,* October 14, 1981.

replacements of cadres."[12] At the ministerial level of construction in Moldavia "the manipulation of systems of direction with two, three, four, and five links has become permanent. During almost the entire 10th Five-Year Plan the *Minstroi* and *Minselstroi* of the Republic were feverish with the shifting of levels."[13]

Hence, it is still "a major objective in the work of Party committees to anchor cadres . . . to reduce their shifting to a minimum." For "experience shows convincingly that the strongest enterprises are those where the same chairman or director is unchangingly at the helm for many years."[14]

The counterpart to inconstancy from above is the famous *tekuchest'* [instability of manpower] from below—those whose occupational career follows the principle "he came and he left,"[15] the "rolling stones" whom the regime has been condemning so strenuously and so vainly for so long.

* * * * * * * *

Even if he stays on the job, a cadre may contribute to unevenness by "throwing himself" or "swaying" from one side or one extreme to the other. "Now they show all-forgivingness and chumminess, and now they are carried away by punishing."[16] A foreman "gives the machine operator one task, and half an hour later he comes running with another."[17] Again, in construction in Moldavia, "there is, on all levels, and with regard to all objects, a desire to build something tomorrow different from that which was planned yesterday. Suppliers have hardly become familiar with one project when another one is proposed to them."[18] (See Chap. II.)

* * * * * * * *

"In the work of particular . . . sectors [of production] breaks still occur; some enterprises fulfill their tasks only irregularly"[19] (see Chap. V)—just as one may observe about a person that "he worked unevenly

---

[12]P. Masherov, speech, "USSR Report: Political and Sociological Affairs," JPRS 76088, pp. 133–148.

[13]Ya. Mogoryan, *P*, September 23, 1981.

[14]L. Kretskov, *P*, December 7, 1982.

[15]M. Krukov, *P*, January 7, 1983.

[16]N. Polozov, *PZh*, 1970, No. 7, p. 39.

[17]A. Komarov, *P*, July 12, 1982.

[18]Ya. Mogoryan, *P*, September 23, 1981.

[19]A. Urov, *PZh*, 1980, No. 3, p. 52.

(*nerovno*),"[20] presumably from cyclical moods (see Chap. I). "A measured rhythm [i.e., evenness] is often absent."[21] For "rhythmical . . . work . . . is often harder for a person or a work collective than brief trials in exceptional circumstances."[22]

Unevenness spreads. "Unsteady delivery of raw materials and materiel raged"[23]—and induced unevenness among users.

Unevenness may be of the second order, affecting those whose mission it is to counteract it. "The work of *kontrol'* over decisions adopted sometimes bears a crash character."[24] (See Chap. I.)

What is required is the opposite. About any task it may be said, "one must not get out of breath. This is a long-run task."[25] "The path to high quality of work is its precise rhythm [i.e., evenness]."[26] "Good work is always also . . . steady work."[27] "V. Grigoriev is an educated engineer given to initiatives . . . but he was excessively hot-headed. . . . Now we never cease to rejoice: look at his even work, without jerks and stoppages."[28] "A true Party worker treats all matters, small or large, with the same seriousness, works with the full giving of his forces independently of the character and the difficulty of the matter at hand."[29]

Such excellence is commensurate with the difficulty of the attainment: "Daily reliability in work . . . is rightly judged heroism."[30]

Evenness of development is a characteristic of socialism in contrast to that basic property of world capitalism, the "uneven development" of its various sectors, its "spasmodic mode of change."[31]

But evenness of performance requires constancy of cadres: "The strongest enterprises are those where the same chairman or director is at the helm unchangingly for many years. . . . The collectives headed by them work evenly, without disruption. . . . "[32]

* * * * * * * *

[20]B. Kachura, *PZh*, No. 16, p. 16.

[21]Editorial, *P*, February 11, 1982.

[22]Editorial, *P*, July 11, 1982.

[23]A. Mendeleev, *PZh*, 1981, No. 2, p. 43.

[24]V. Kozhenyako, PZh, 1979, No. 20, p. 29.

[25]Yu. Andropov, in a factory, no date, *P*, February 1, 1983.

[26]Editorial, *P*, February 11, 1982.

[27]Editorial, *P*, March 12, 1982.

[28]V. Musin, *P*, March 22, 1982.

[29]K. Chernenko 1980, p. 290.

[30]Editorial, *P*, July 11, 1982.

[31]A. Gromyko, *MEMO*, 1983, No. 4, p. 18.

[32]L. Kretskov, *P*, December 7, 1982.

Unevenness is, in the view of the Party leadership, linked to anxiety; evenness, to its absence, to calm (whose other shade of meaning, low activeness, is disapproved; see Chap. I). This may present the deceptive appearance of a disapproved slowness: "Calm in every circumstance, he seemed at first sight even to be slow."[33]

The dread alternative to calm in a crisis is being overwhelmed with anxiety and so incapable of effective action. "In weak persons difficulties . . . sometimes provoke the feeling of losing their bearings."[34] "Faced with caprices of nature, many cadres in agriculture lose their bearings."[35]

In contrast, "every step of ours must be calm";[36] what is required is "the creation of a genuinely calm . . . atmosphere in all spheres of our activity."[37]

Calm rather than excited bustle in normal circumstances is a mark of excellence. "The everyday activity of the Party District Committee in Rossoshansk is characterized by calm work by all members."[38]

Calm rather than unmastered anxiety in crisis is a virtue of the highest order. Upon an accident in a factory, "the brigade does not lose its bearings."[39] "He directed the battle with utmost calm."[40] "Only Kuzmin kept his calm."[41]

Calm rather than ungoverned elation in success is nearly as important. "What I most remember is his calm. Something does not work out, the plan is disrupted—Anatolyi Nikolaevich is outwardly unperturbed. We are successful—again he is calm."[42] Thus calm is also evenness.

---

[33]L. Brezhnev, *Malaya Zemla*, Brezhnev 1979, p. 31.

[34]N. Konovalov, *PZh*, April 1980, No. 7, p. 55.

[35]P. Masherov, *P*, June 15, 1980.

[36]V. Vorotnikov, *PZh*, 1975, No. 14, p. 11.

[37]K. Chernenko 1980, p. 303.

[38]V. Vorotnikov, *PZh*, 1975, No. 14, p. 11.

[39]R. Sabirov, *P*, October 3, 1980.

[40]L. Brezhnev, *Malaya Zemla*, Brezhnev 1979, p. 39.

[41]Op. cit., p. 26.

[42]Op. cit., p. 10.

Chapter VIII

LACK OF COHESION (*RAZOBSHCHENNOST'*)

The Party leadership believes, I conjecture, that members of a collective are apt to be indifferent toward one another (Chap. I), and hence to "act apart in the collective,"[1] with the effect of reducing the common yield. There is an inclination to adopt "an attitude of this-does-not-concern-me with regard to the affairs of others, to react with indifference toward events that do not directly touch narrowly personal interests."[2] "The member of a collective who takes up the position of an observer from the sidelines looks indifferently at the evil that touches somebody else. What does it matter if everything around him burns!"[3] "*Odin v pole ne voin* [a fighter is not alone on the battlefield]—not all understand this fully."[4] In the reconstruction of a factory after the War "there was no cooperation."[5]

Against such dispositions the Party leadership requires "the capacity to be concerned with 'alien' affairs."[6]

Beyond indifference within the collective there is, if "things are left to themselves," hostility: "squabbles, slander, anonymous letters corrode the collective."[7] "At a meeting of related groups of workers (*smezhnik*) within a factory, they began, as often happens, to unload responsibility from the one to the other."[8] "How do we usually behave? When we have seen something going wrong, yelling erupts. . . . "[9] In the reconstruction of the factory remembered by Brezhnev, "there were endless quarrels, mutual accusations."[10] When "in the manager the administrator comes to prevail over the educator, . . . many mutual offenses and protracted conflicts occur."[11]

---

[1]E. Kachalovskii, *PZh*, 1981, No. 18, p. 28.

[2]Unsigned article, *K*, 1982, No. 2, p. 49.

[3]V. Lebedeva, *P*, January 14, 1982.

[4]K. Umarov, *P*, October 12, 1981.

[5]L. Brezhnev, *Vozrozhdenie*, Brezhnev 1979, p. 64.

[6]B. Golovets, *P*, January 12, 1982.

[7]V. Vasilets, *P*, December 9, 1981.

[8]M. Kryukov, *P*, October 10, 1981.

[9]V. Sidorelko, quoted by V. Lisin, *P*, September 29, 1982.

[10]*Vozrozhdenie*, L. Brezhnev 1979, p. 9.

[11]A manager, quoted by V. Ivanov, *P*, January 22, 1980.

In these conditions it becomes appropriate for "enterprises to arrange for their cooperation in work under the slogan: 'From mutual grudges to mutual help.'"[12] Thus there was an "appeal of the advanced brigades at the Moscow factory in the name of Vladimir Ilyich to go over from mutual grudges to mutual help."[13]

Little is needed for internal war to erupt. "The smallest mistake can provoke complications in the collective, discord among workers."[14]

Hence, "there is often talk . . . in Party meetings . . . of how relations between persons within brigades develop, so that the smallest lack of understanding or of clarity can be nipped immediately"[15] before it develops into a large and destructive force.

* * * * * * *

To counter the tendency for a collective to disintegrate, the Party promotes norms that favor cohesion. "In any collective people of different ages, characters, and qualifications are working. To create a comradely atmosphere among them is not a simple task. In a series of . . . enterprises . . . 'codes of workers' honor' have been established in which the moral-ethical and operational relationships among the members of the collective are specified. Conformity to such a code is placed under . . . *kontrol'*."[16]

The Party leadership favors arrangements that place the desired performance of others in my own interest, and mine in theirs. That is the point of the work brigade: "The former attitudes—'this is not my affair, not my concern'—are now inapplicable for us."[17] For now operates "the principle of the collective moral *and material* responsibility for work discipline and public order. . . . For each violation of discipline or of public order the entire collective now bears responsibility."[18] "When the metal worker Ch. was not admitted to work by the brigadier because of drunkenness, his comrades were forced to perform his work task. And . . . they were deprived of 5 percent of their premiums. . . . The brigade . . . forced the guilty one to answer for his deed. . . . Since then there have been no violations here for a long time."[19]

---

[12]Editorial, *P*, January 3, 1981.

[13]Editorial, *PZh*, 1980, No. 16, p. 5.

[14]M. Gusev, *K*, 1979, No. 12, p. 55.

[15]A. Muzyrya, *K*, 1980, No. 14, p. 31.

[16]V. Ignatov, *PZh*, 1976, No. 24, p. 31.

[17]A brigadier, quoted by B. Evladov, *P*, December 8, 1981.

[18]I. Vasiliev, *P*, November 19, 1981. Emphasis added.

[19]V. Ivanov, *P*, April 12, 1980.

* * * * * * * *

Indifference and hostility may induce one to leave the collective (Chap. VII). "Research indicates that the majority of departures of personnel in a series of enterprises are not due to insufficiency of salary, but because relations did not work out."[20]

Or one may remain in the collective while working by oneself as much as feasible; certainly, then, keeping one's distinctive skills to oneself—against which the Party leadership unceasingly insists on "sharing advanced experience," "generously sharing one's knowledge with comrades."[21] "It is particularly important that innovators not keep their discoveries a secret. . . . "[22]

"Eagerly sharing one's experience"[23] is praiseworthy. In a model enterprise "no silence is kept about the secrets of high skill."[24] A model worker "for the last few years generously transmitted to about forty young workers the secrets of his high skill."[25] To the instructor of the Buryat Province Committee of the Party, Vladimir Georgievich Bolshakov, "sincere gratitude was expressed . . . by many secretaries of primary Party organizations and workers of district and city committees of the Party. They thank him for having generously shared all that he learned in the course of many years of work in the economy, in the soviets, and in the Party."[26]

* * * * * * * *

Indifference and hostility toward other members of one's group combine to reduce the level of performance on which they all depend, and thus to create the sense of "letting them down"—a sense that may extend to impersonal entities: "So That Technology [Will] Not Let Them Down (*Shtoby Tekhnika ne Podvela).*"[27]

Members of a collective may refuse to come to the aid of one another in dire straits. It is against such a refusal that the Party leadership stresses the requirement of "readiness to give support to a comrade at any moment."[28] "Every work cell should be characterized by . . . mutual help."[29]

---

[20]D. Senin, *P*, April 8, 1982.

[21]Editorial, *P*, September 10, 1981.

[22]A. Brygin, *K*, 1982, No. 15, p. 61.

[23]N. Kaparin, *P*, August 6, 1981.

[24]Editorial, *P*, January 16, 1982.

[25]R. Kondratyuk, *PZh*, 1977, No. 13, p. 64.

[26]Editorial, *P*, September 15, 1981.

[27]Headline, *P*, January 7, 1983.

[28]K. Chernenko 1978, p. 108.

[29]Op. cit., p. 23.

The propensity to render aid to associates in distress, so far from emerging spontaneously, has to be called into existence and maintained by seemingly unrelated measures. "All this," it may be said of many an action, "builds in the souls of people such traits as . . . the readiness to aid a comrade in need."[30]

Stress may be laid on the ulterior benefits accruing from such conduct. "Mutual help" may change failure into success: "It [sometimes] happens that favorable indicators hide unfavorable developments. . . . The inverse also happens. . . . In a collective where until now nothing has gladdened [the spirits], favorable changes occur, mutual help is growing—and that leads to qualitative changes in production."[31] "When in a collective . . . an atmosphere of harmony and of mutual help reigns, then things go well."[32]

Mutual help is a supreme quality, to be proclaimed by a tautology—"a friend will always support you"[33]—or by what is at best a truism—"the firmer the cohesion of the collective, the stronger mutual support."[34] "In such a collective," one writes about a model brigade, "everybody willingly helps out the neighbor."[35] "They created an atmosphere in the shift in which the slogan 'one for all, and all for one' is realized not in words, but in fact."[36] "We metal workers have an unwritten law . . . to help each other. If you violate that law, don't expect success. Ivan Grigorevich Gachegov follows this remarkable principle strictly."[37]

Setting at least a verbal example for the "masses" seemingly disinclined to help, the Party calls any act that has a nonenemy as its target an act of *pomoshch'*, or help—as undesired perhaps by that target as the Party's interference might be.

* * * * * * * *

According to the Party leadership, in my reading of the matter, a work collective's "cohesion [*splochennost'*, *slazhennost'*, *soglasovannost'*, *vzaimodeistvie*]" depends sharply on good feelings within the collective prevailing over indifference, hostility, divergence.

---

[30]G. Krivoshein, *PZh*, 1979, No. 16, p. 40.

[31]V. Ivanov, *P*, April 12, 1980.

[32]V. Gusev, *P*, February 19, 1982.

[33]Headline, *P*, April 17, 1980.

[34]G. Krivoshein, *PZh*, 1979, No. 16, p. 38.

[35]A. Muzyrya, *K*, 1980, No. 14, p. 32.

[36]V. Sapov, *P*, January 19, 1980.

[37]R. Kondratyuk, *PZh*, 1977, No. 13, p. 64.

Yet such a condition seems to be considered one of rare excellence. "In the area of Smolensk the Talashkin poultry-breeding farm enjoys a good reputation. . . . People live there like an harmonious [*druzhno*] family."[38]

If cohesion depends sharply on good feelings, the collective's yield in turn depends sharply on its cohesion. "When a collective is *druzhen* and *slazhen*, all difficulties are removed."[39]

Yet high cohesion of a collective is an excellence worth stressing, as is the high inner cohesion of a person. "This collective is not large, but *druzhen*."[40] "This collective is famous for its capacity to work harmoniously. . . . "[41] "The Central Committee, its Politburo and Secretariat," so runs a claim unabashedly made by members of these bodies themselves, "is a collective that is *slazhennyi, druzhnyi*."[42]

The Party leadership, I conjecture, believes that if the yield of a collective is not to be low, its cohesion must be *very* high. "Our class enemies know very well what the unity of the Party means. . . . G. Kennan wrote: 'If somebody . . . succeeded in impairing the unity . . . of the Communist Party, Soviet Russia might quickly be transformed from one of the strongest societies into one of the weakest and most insignificant.'"[43]

Hence, all members of the Party must keep "acting . . . as one person."[44] "Party organizations strive to obtain cohesion [*splochenie*] of their collectives . . . the capacity to work, as one says, *with one breath*."[45] "When the members of an elected organ [of the Party] act with cohesion [*slazhenno*], *as one person. . . .* "[46]

Through the link just indicated, the yield of a collective *sharply* depends on the feelings of its members toward each other. "What, then, is the major factor making for the success of the best Party organizations and work collectives? Every time one convinces oneself: affairs go well there where people live and work *druzhno*"[47]—a word spanning the area between friendship and mere propriety.

---

[38]I. Klimenko, *P*, February 11, 1982.

[39]A worker, quoted in *P*, January 12, 1980.

[40]V. Agapov, *PZh*, 1980, No. 16, p. 23.

[41]Editorial, *P*, April 28, 1983.

[42]K. Chernenko 1978, p. 27.

[43]Editorial, *K*, 1982, No. 18, pp. 8–9.

[44]Ibid.

[45]G. Krivoshein, *PZh*, 1979, No. 16, p. 39. Emphasis added.

[46]Editorial, *P*, December 26, 1980.

[47]Editorial, *P*, January 16, 1982.

If cohesion needs to be very high for yield not to be low, feelings may also have to be very good for cohesion to be very high. High yield may thus come to depend on *edinodeistvie* [the collective acting as one], which depends in turn on *edinodushie* [the collective having but one soul]: "*edinodushie* and *splochennost'* [cohesion]."[48] Divergence first in spirit and then in conduct destroys yield: "The opportunist groups [in the Party's past] pushed the Party toward a split. They wanted to reduce the leading role of the Party to nothing."[49]

If a collective's yield depends sharply on its cohesion and that on feelings within it, these in turn *sharply* depend on the Party counteracting the "spontaneous" tendency toward bad feelings/low cohesion. It is "the task of the primary Party organization" to "make people cohere into a collective capable of work";[50] it is the primary Party organization which must create "an atmosphere of cohesive work in the collective."[51] "One must always remember that the primary Party organizations are the *main . . . force . . . in the creation in every collective of an atmosphere of work. . . . Primary Party organizations must constantly* be concerned with creating in every collective an atmosphere of work. . . . "[52] To show the excellence of a leader, one may observe that "he . . . was able to give cohesion to newly formed collectives."[53]

Ultimately, then, the yield of a collective depends on the Party: an assertion whose convenience should prevent it from being fully disbelieved within the Party—like so many affirmations discussed in these pages.

---

[48]V. Shcherbitskii 1978, p. 224.

[49]A. Pelshe, speech, May 16, 1975, Pelshe 1978, p. 578.

[50]Editorial, *PZh*, 1980, No. 16, p. 19.

[51]Unsigned article, *PZh*, 1976, No. 23, p. 40.

[52]Editorial, *PZh*, 1981, No. 19, p. 4. Emphasis added.

[53]Editorial, *P*, February 10, 1981.

Chapter IX

SUPERIORS' RAGE AND REMOTENESS (*GRUBOST', BEZUCHAST'NOST'*)

"Not for nothing does every letter from the District to the Province Committee of the Party speak of the inattentiveness of leaders to the needs of people."[1] Statements of this kind are frequent; they seem to show that the leadership views officials' detachment from their subordinates as a factor that seriously degrades mood and hence performance.

Even more does this criticism apply to superiors' outbursts of rage against those under them. "Not for nothing," the same observer adds, "does every second letter from the District to the Province committee of the Party speak of the rudeness of leaders."[2]

So widespread and damaging is such conduct that it provokes an often and strongly voiced demand to abstain from it. "To have the right to lead a collective, one must possess one important quality—to behave respectfully toward people."[3] One must not reduce *kontrol'* to a 'general dressing down.'"[4] At province Party conferences "it would be wrong to utilize the platform merely for 'dressing-down.'"[5]

Lack of rudeness to subordinates draws praise. In particular, praise attaches to the capacity to keep the quality of exactingness free of rudeness: "Vladimir Grigorievich is exacting toward his subordinates, *but* his exactingness is associated with a respectful attitude to every human being. . . . "[6] "I don't know a single case . . . in which Galina Petrovna [a cadre] offended somebody by a sharp word."[7]

* * * * * * * *

Whoever abundantly expresses rage toward subordinates whom he deems defenseless may, in turn, intensely fear inducing rage in inferiors, peers, and superiors whom he considers capable of retaliating. He may in the second case abstain from a sharpness of conduct which the objective at hand requires. "The managers in a series of

[1]V. Vrozd, *P*, December 15, 1982.

[2]Ibid.

[3]Editorial, *P*, February 16, 1983.

[4]A. Litovchenko, *P*, July 27, 1981.

[5]Editorial, *P*, December 12, 1980.

[6]S. Vasyutin, *PZh*, 1980, No. 6, p. 55. Emphasis added.

[7]A worker, quoted in an editorial, *P*, May 18, 1983.

enterprises . . . strive 'to offend nobody.' In these conditions, [the] intensive . . . work of workers showing high initiative is equated, as to remuneration, with the work of those who do not always fulfill their . . . obligations. . . . "[8] "In some committees, when colliding with a sharp question . . . there is a striving to smooth angles . . . to reconcile the 'sides.'"[9] There are "persons who . . . try to smooth out and make a detour around unsolved problems, who keep silent about sharp questions."[10] "They simply do not want to spoil their relations with anybody." "The first secretary of the district committee of the Party, I. Dotsenko, as a matter of principle, did not criticize anybody and did not wish to be criticized either."[11] "Nobody offends anybody and all are content with all."[12] Only the Kremlin is not. "Neither conflict nor quarrels—peace and harmony. Do we need such happiness?"[13]

---

[8]Editorial, *K*, 1974, No. 11, p. 12.

[9]Editorial, *P*, January 6, 1982.

[10]M. Suslov, *K*, 1979, No. 15, p. 33.

[11]S. Manyakin, *PZh*, 1979, No. 10, p. 40.

[12]M. Suslov, *K*, 1979, No. 15, p. 36.

[13]K. Bondarenko, *P*, September 3, 1980.

Chapter X

FEAR AND FEAR OF FEAR (*STRAKH*)

Each chapter above has dealt with a possibly distinctive fear of the Kremlin as to how the conduct of cadres, of "masses," and of itself may go wrong—leading to what the Soviet leadership, I surmise, in spoken or silent thought, calls the threat of annihilation. To the situation of 1918–1919 and 1941–1942—and tomorrow?

The preceding pages have also, it seems to me, shown the Kremlin's fear of fear: how the leadership avoids expressing its fears while straining to combat them. The very words closest to fear are nearly banned from public use: caution [*ostorozhnost'*], danger [*opasnost'*, *ugroza*], fear itself [*strakh*, *boyazn'*], annihilation [*gibel'*], and death [*smert'*].

REFERENCES

K	*Kommunist* (fortnightly)
P	*Pravda* (daily)
PZh	*Partiinaya Zhizn'* (fortnightly)
--	*Voprosy Istorii KPSS* (monthly)

Brezhnev, L. I. (1979a)	Leninskim kursom, Vol. 1, Moscow, Politizdat
Brezhnev, L. I. (1970b)	Leninskim kursom, Vol. 2
Brezhnev, L. I. (1972)	Leninskim kursom, Vol. 3
Brezhnev, L. I. (1974)	Leninskim kursom, Vol. 4
Brezhnev, L. I. (1976)	Leninskim kursom, Vol. 5
Brezhnev, L. I. (1978)	Leninskim kursom, Vol. 6
Brezhnev, L. I. (1979)	Leninskim kursom, Vol. 7
Brezhnev, L. I. (1981a)	Leninskim kursom, Vol. 8
Brezhnev, L. I. (198lb)	Vospominaniya, *Novy mir* 1981, No. 111 pp. 1–26.
Chernenko, K. U. (1978)	Nekotorye voprosy tvorcheskogo razvitiya stilya partiinoi i gosudarstvennoi raboty, Moscow, Politizdat
Chernenko, K. U. (1980)	Voprosy raboty partiinogo i gosudarstvennogo apparata, Moscow Politizdat
Grishin, V. V. (1979)	Izbrannye rechi i stat'i, Moscow Politizdat
Pelshe, A. R. (1978)	Izbrannye rechi i stat'i, Moscow Politizdat
Shcherbitskii, V. V. (1978)	Ovladevat' leninskim stilem raboty, Kiev, Politizdat Ukrainy
Ustinov, D. F. (1979)	Izbrannye rechi i stat'i, Moscow Politizdat.

INDEX

Absenteeism, 42, 50
Action: need for uninterrupted, 80–82; words and, 65–69. *See also* Inaction
Activating as chief task, 15–16, 17–18
Activeness (*aktivnost'*), 4–18; appearance of, 6; Central Committee and, 79; and completing a job, 62–63; criticism and, 14–15; heightening 14–15; success and, 12–13
Agitators, activating the, 15
Agriculture, 22–23, 93; Party role in, 2
Aktivnost'. *See* Activeness
Alcohol, 50, 102
Analysis. *See* Discussions
Andropov, Yu. V., 36, 37, 49–50, 67, 75
Antonovich, I. A., 61
Anxiety, 100
Arms, gestures of, 60
Avtoremles, 95

Bezdeistvie. *See* Inaction
Borisov, 6
Brezhnev, Leonid Ilyich, 7, 11, 13, 19, 23, 25, 29, 34, 44, 64, 74, 89, 97, 101
"Brigade" system, 42, 44, 49, 51, 94, 97, 102
Bureau of City Committee, 66
Bureaucratism, 2, 40

Calmness, 100
Central Committee of CPSU, 3, 12; activeness and, 79; May 1982 Plenum, 79; November 1971 Plenum, 89; role in activating masses, 17–18. *See also* Party Congresses
Change, aversion to, 28–29
Cohesion: good feelings and, 104–106; lack of, 101–106
Common cause, 34, 40, 45; appeal of, 31–32; as production incentive, 32, 33. *See also* Selflessness
Communist Party of the Soviet Union (CPSU). *See* Central Committee of CPSU; Party; Party Congresses
Competency, 52–53
Complacency, 12–13
Complaints, 40
Completing the job, 58–76
Concentration: importance of, 77–79; of forces, 87
Concern, lack of, 10
Conferences, 66
Conformity, obtaining, 39
Conscience, 57; and *kontrol'*, 55
Construction work, 64–65, 74–76; completion of, 73–74; "storming" in, 85
Contracts, violation of, 37
Control. *See Kontrol'*
Cooperation, 102
Criticism, 107–108; activeness and, 14–15

Deadlines, 85
Decisionmaking, *kontrol'* and, 52, 54
Decisions: forgetting, 69–70; implementing, 59–60, 70–72, 72–74; need for definiteness, 90–92; resources and, 92–95
Defects in products, 73–74
Definiteness, 90–92
Delays, 86
Delegation of work, 74
Discipline, 35, 56, 102
Discussions, 65–69
Disorder, 36
Documentation, 69
Dolg' (duty), 30–40, 62; fulfillment of, 34; income and, 44; *kontrol'* vs., 54, 57; performance, income, and, 46; work as, 33
Drinking, 50, 102
Duty. *See* Dolg'

Ease, as avoidance of initiative, 26–27
Economic incentives, 40–51
Economic outcomes, Party role in, 1–4
Economy, 68
Education: by *kontrol'*, 55; of economic managers, 39

Efficiency (*delovitost'*), 11
Elation: need for permanent, 25; and productivity, 19; work and, 23–24
Energy conservation, 65
Engineers, 45
Enthusiasm: arousing, 22–23; for work, 25
Equipment: defective, 9; disorder and, 36
Ereva, A. I., 6
Estimates, 89, 95
Estonia, 91
Exactingness: need for, 14; rudeness and, 107; talk of, 68
Excuses, 10

Factories, 74, 87
Failures, 56; lack of preparation and, 95–96; to calculate, 89–96; to complete job, 58–76
Farms, 10
Fear: Kremlin's fear of, 109; performance and, 54–55
Feelings: importance of, 105–106; productivity and, 19. *See also* Mood
Five Year Plans, 2, 37, 65, 75, 83, 86, 98

German Democratic Republic, 36
Gestures, 60; arm spreading, 9–10; arm waving, 10; shrugging, 10
Glavpromostroi of Krasnodar, 5
Goals, 90; *kontrol'* and accomplishing, 53
Golovin, Aleksandr Andreevich, 19

Habit of working, 33
Happiness, 108
Helplessness, expressions of, 9–10, 60
Hostility, 101, 103

Ideals, 55
Ilyich, Vladimir, 102
Inaction (*bezdeistvie*), 1–57; dangers of, 7–12; decisions and, 72; urge to, 83, 84. *See also* Action; Activeness
Income: immorality of striving for, 50; work and, 32. *See also* Wages
Indifference, 9–10, 12, 70, 101, 102, 103; of managers to moods, 21–22; overcoming, 11; toward work, 24
Inefficiency, overlooking, 9, 10. *See also* Surveillance
Inertia, 28–29; elimination of, 13
Initiative: as need, 34; lack of, 7
Inspiration: economic performance and, 20; success and, 20
Intermittence (*preryvistost'*), 80–82

Kapultsevich, V., 6
Kiev, 10
Kontrol' (control), 5, 51–57; conformity to code, 102; education and, 55; job completion and, 58, 59; need for concreteness, 91–92; performance and, 52–53; weakening of, 12
Krasnyi Bogatyr, 2
Kuznets Metallurgical Kombinat, 88

Leadership: activeness and, 13; conduct and, 107–108; job completion and, 58–59. *See also* Managers; Party leadership
Leniency, 13
Lenin, Vladimir Ilyich, 7, 11, 29, 30, 65–66
Likhachev, Ivan Alekseevich, 11
Lithuania, 90

Machinery, 93
Magnitogorsk, 38–39
Malikov, F., 69
Management, need for calculation, 89–96
Managers: broken promises and, 60–62; concern with moods of people, 21–22; discussions and, 66–69; *kontrol'* and, 54, 55, 56; and new modes of production, 28–29; penalties, 42
Marx, Karl, 29
Marxist–Leninist theory, 5
Material stimulation, Party leadership views on, 43–51
Maximizing work, 32–33
Mediocrity (*obyvatel'*), 12
Meetings, 68–69
Ministry of Agricultural Machinebuilding, 9
Ministry of Finance, 42
Ministry of Industrial Construction, 87
Ministry of Sovkhozes, 10

Mobility, 44
Moldavia, 98
Mood: for work, 50; Party's mastery over, 20–21; productivity and, 19–20. *See also* Feelings
Morality, 55
Mozoloyako, M. I., 61

Neprodumannost' (failure to calculate), 89–96
Neravnodushi. See Nonindifference
Nerovnost'. See Unevenness
Nonindifference, 10; and power over events, 11
Novosibirsk factory, 86

Obligations, 37–38. *See also* Dolg'
Orderliness, need for, 38
Organization: discussions and, 68; lack of, 35

Party: demands of people, 38–39; educating people to work 34, 38–39; levels of *kontrol'*, 56–57; role in economy, 1–4
Party building, school of, 15
Party Congresses, 13, 29, 35, 66, 79, 97
Party leadership: disapproval of aspiration to earn more, 46–48; emphasis on attaining objectives, 63–64; views on material stimulation, 43–51; views on work discipline, 102
Party meetings, 15
Party organization, activation within, 15–17
Passivity, 9–10, 12; causes, 14–15; exactingness and, 14; leniency and, 13
Pay, piece-work, 42–43. *See also* Wages
Penalties, 50
Performance: fear and, 54–55; income and, 42–43; *kontrol'* and, 52–57; need for uninterrupted action, 80–82; and striving for income, 48–49; wasting time, 83–88. *See also* Work performance
Planning: estimating, 95; and failure to calculate, 89–96; feasibility in, 94–95; need for, 91–92; phases of operation, 59; time requirements, 83–88
Pod'em (surge), income benefits and, 44–45
Pokaznaya ispolnitel'nost', 6
Political information specialists, 15
Power to influence events, 11
Premiums, 45
Preryvistost'. See Intermittence
Productivity: elation and, 19; failure to improve, 70; good feelings and, 105; importance of mood, 21–23; mutual help and, 103–104; Party role in, 1–4; *pod'em* in, 23; salaries and, 41; socialism and, 32; speed, 13, 86–88; working conditions and, 20
Products, defective, 73–74, 85
Promises: fulfilling, 60–62; unfulfilled, 75–76
Prosperity, work as source of, 32
Province Committee, 16–17, 18
Punctuality, 88
Purposefulness, 90–92

Railways, 87
Raspylenie. See Scattering
Razobshchennost'. See Cohesion, lack of
Research, 64
Responsibility: attitude of, 37; heightening sense of, 55, 56; lack of, 35; teaching, 39
Routine, preference for, 28–29
Rudeness of leaders, 107–108
"Running in place," 6

Salaries, production and, 41. *See also* Wages
Samotek, 58
Scattering (*raspylenie*), 74–76, 77–79
Scheduling, 83–88. *See also* Planning
Scientists, performance and income, 43
Selflessness, 31–32, 40, 50; as requirement, 39. *See also* Common cause
Shchekin method, 51
Socialism, production and, 32
Specialists: enthusiasm for work 45; *kontrol'* and, 54; R&D, 7
Speed, 86; importance of not losing, 13
Spontaneity, 58, 82, 83; preparation and, 95–96
Stikhia. See Spontaneity
"Storming," 85

Strakh. *See* Fear
Stubbornness, 63–64
Success: activeness and, 12–13; complacency and, 12–13; inspiration and, 20; mutual help and, 104
Supervision, 107–108. *See also* Leadership; Managers
Surge (*pod'em*), 18–30
Surveillance (*kontrolirovat'*), 14, 51–57

Tardiness, 84
Team method, 51
Technology, introduction of, 42, 56
Time requirements, 83–88
Tomkabel, 86

Underestimating one's capacities, 9–10
Unevenness (*nerovnost'*), 97–100
Unity, need for, 105

Vacations, 44
Vedomstvennost'. *See* Bureaucratism
Violations, 39, 56, 61, 102; of contracts, 36–37; intolerance of, 39–40; *kontrol'* and, 53

Wages: dependent on input, 45; Party's views on, 43–51; role in stimulating workers, 42–43. *See also* Income; Salaries
Wasting time, 83–88
Work: as basis for life, 24; as beauty, 34; as debt, 30; as duty, 33; as habit, 34–35; as inner need, 34, 35, 39; as source of joy, 33; deterioration from too little, 34; discussions and, 65–68; dragging out, 86–88; economic incentives to, 40–51; fraud and, 49; increasing productivity, 29; maximizing, 32–33; new methods of, 63; "only for the ruble," 46–49
Work conditions, 20
Work mood (*trudovoi nastroi*), 19. *See also* Mood
Work performance: cohesion and, 104–106; elation and, 25–26; mood and, 21–23, 25; steadiness in, 97–100. *See also* Performance
Work relay, 88

SELECTED LIST OF RAND BOOKS

Becker, Abraham S. *Military Expenditure Limitation for Arms Control: Problems and Prospects, With a Documentary History of Recent Proposals.* Cambridge, Mass.: Ballinger Publishing Company. 1977.

Becker, Abraham S. *Soviet National Income, 1958-1964: National Accounts of the USSR in the Seven Year Plan Period.* Berkeley and Los Angeles: University of California Press, 1969.

Brewer, Garry D., and Martin Shubik. *The War Game: A Critique of Military Problem Solving.* Cambridge, Mass.: Harvard University Press, 1979.

Curry, Jane L. (trans. and ed.). *The Black Book of Polish Censorship.* New York: Random House, Inc., 1984.

Dinerstein, H. S. *War and the Soviet Union: Nuclear Weapons and the Revolution in Soviet Military and Political Thinking.* New York: Frederick A. Praeger, Inc., 1959. (Reprint Edition: Westport, Conn.: Greenwood Press, 1976.)

Goldhamer, Herbert. *The Adviser.* New York: Elsevier North-Holland, Inc., 1978.

Goldhamer, Herbert. *The Soviet Soldier: Soviet Military Management at the Troop Level.* New York: Crane, Russak & Company, Inc., 1975.

Goldhamer, Herbert, and Andrew W. Marshall. *Psychosis and Civilization.* Glencoe, Ill.: The Free Press, 1953. (Reprint Edition: Salem, N.H.: Ayer Co., 1979.)

Hosmer, Stephen T., Konrad Kellen, and Brian M. Jenkins. *The Fall of South Vietnam: Statements by Vietnamese Military and Civilian Leaders.* New York: Crane, Russak & Company, Inc., 1980.

Hsieh, Alice Langley. *Communist China's Strategy in the Nuclear Era.* Englewood Cliffs, N.J.: Prentice-Hall, Inc., 1962. (Reprint Edition: Westport, Conn.: Greenwood Press, 1976.)

Janis, Irving L. *Air War and Emotional Stress: Psychological Studies of Bombing and Civilian Defense.* New York: McGraw-Hill Book Company, Inc., 1951. (Reprint Edition: Westport, Conn.: Greenwood Press, 1976.)

Johnson, A. Ross, Robert W. Dean, and Alexander Alexiev. *East European Military Establishments: The Warsaw Pact Northern Tier.* New York: Crane, Russak & Company, Inc., 1982.

Langer, Paul F., and Joseph J. Zasloff. *North Vietnam and the Pathet Lao: Partners in the Struggle for Laos.* Cambridge, Mass.: Harvard University Press, 1970.

Leites, Nathan. *The Operational Code of the Politburo.* New York: McGraw-Hill Book Company, Inc., 1951. (Reprint Edition: Westport, Conn.: Greenwood Press, 1972.)

Leites, Nathan. *Soviet Style in War.* New York: Crane, Russak & Company, Inc., 1982.

Leites, Nathan. *A Study of Bolshevism.* Glencoe, Ill.: The Free Press, 1953.

Pye, Lucian. *Chinese Commercial Negotiating Style.* Cambridge, Mass.: Oelgeschlager, Gunn & Hain, Publishers, Inc., 1982.

Pye, Lucian. *The Dynamics of Chinese Politics.* Cambridge, Mass.: Oelgeschlager, Gunn & Hain, Publishers, Inc., 1981.

Robinson, Thomas W. (ed.). *The Cultural Revolution in China.* Berkeley and Los Angeles: University of California Press, 1971.

Rush, Myron. *Political Succession in the USSR.* New York: Columbia University Press, 1965.

Solomon, Richard H. (ed.). *Asian Security in the 1980s: Problems and Policies for a Time of Transition.* Cambridge, Mass.: Oelgeschlager, Gunn & Hain, Publishers, Inc., 1980.

Whiting, Allen S. *China Crosses the Yalu: The Decision to Enter the Korean War.* New York: The Macmillan Company, 1960. Stanford, Calif.: Stanford University Press, 1968.

Wolfe, Thomas W. *The SALT Experience.* Cambridge, Mass.: Ballinger Publishing Company, 1979.

Wolfe, Thomas W. *Soviet Power and Europe, 1945–1970.* Baltimore, Md.: The Johns Hopkins Press, 1970.